PASTA RECIPES

An Easy Pasta Cookbook for Your Gathering

(Greatest Pasta Cookbook of All Time)

Norman Hecht

Published by Alex Howard

© **Norman Hecht**

All Rights Reserved

Pasta Recipes: An Easy Pasta Cookbook for Your Gathering (Greatest Pasta Cookbook of All Time)

ISBN 978-1-990169-07-6

All rights reserved. No part of this guide may be reproduced in any form without permission in writing from the publisher except in the case of brief quotations embodied in critical articles or reviews.

Legal & Disclaimer

The information contained in this book is not designed to replace or take the place of any form of medicine or professional medical advice. The information in this book has been provided for educational and entertainment purposes only.

The information contained in this book has been compiled from sources deemed reliable, and it is accurate to the best of the Author's knowledge; however, the Author cannot guarantee its accuracy and validity and cannot be held liable for any errors or omissions. Changes are periodically made to this book. You must consult your doctor or get professional medical advice before using any of the suggested remedies, techniques, or information in this book.

Table of contents

PART 1 1

INTRODUCTION 2

Anchovy Tomato and Mushroom Pasta Recipe 4
Arugula Pesto and Pine Nuts Pasta Recipe 6
Baked Macaroni with Turkey and Cheese Recipe 7
Easy Beef and Zucchini Lasagna Recipe 9
Minced Turkey in Tomato Sauce with Herbs Recipe 10
Easy Pasta ala Vongole in White Wine Sauce Recipe 12
Spaghetti with Meatball Sauce and Parmesan Recipe 14
Spaghetti Carbonara with Roasted Turkey and Herbs Recipe 16
Spicy Spaghetti with Prawns and Herbs Recipe 18
Tagliatelle with Tuna in Pesto Sauce Recipe 19
Spaghetti with Straw Mushroom and Spinach Recipe 21
Creamy Mushroom Pasta with Paprika Recipe 22
Baked Mac and Cheese Recipe 24
Baked Ziti with Meat in Tomato Sauce Recipe 25
Creamy Pasta with Zucchini and Mushroom Recipe 27
Fettuccini with Shrimp Lemon and Parsley Recipe 28
Italian Seafood Pasta Recipe 30
Pasta Salmon and Cheese Casserole Recipe 32
Penne with Minced Meat in Tomato Sauce Recipe 33
Fettuccini with Creamy Mushroom Sauce Recipe 35
Fusilli with Salmon and Spinach in Cream Sauce Recipe 37
Herbed Artichoke Pasta with Parmesan Recipe 38
Creamy Mac and Cheese Recipe 39
Chicken Lasagna with Bechamel Sauce Recipe 41
Pasta with Alfredo Sauce Recipe 44
Seafood Pasta with Fresh Parmesan Recipe 45
Pasta with Mixed Vegetables Stir Fry Recipe 47
Pasta with Sun-Dried Tomatoes and Anchovies Recipe 48
Penne with Chicken in White Sauce Recipe 50
Penne with Eggplant Tomato and Basil Recipe 52

Spaghetti with Meat and Veggies in Tomato Sauce Recipe 53
Spaghetti in Pesto Sauce with Parmesan Recipe 55
Cumin Spiced Spaghetti Puttanesca Recipe 56
Spaghetti with Asparagus and Cherry Tomatoes Recipe 58
Spaghetti with Stewed Tomatoes Basil and Garlic Recipe 59
Veggie and Pasta Medley Recipe 61
Tagliatelle with Spinach Pesto and Peas Recipe 62
Tagliatelle with Seafood in Tomato Sauce Recipe 63
Spaghetti with Meat and Mushroom Recipe 65
Roasted Chicken Vegetable and Pasta Salad 67
Easy Macaroni and Vegetable Salad Recipe 68
Tuna Pasta Salad Recipe with Yogurt-Herb Dressing 69
Pasta with Feta Tomato and Pepper Recipe 70
Spaghetti with Tomato Feta and Olives Recipe 72
Tuna Corn and Pasta Salad Recipe 73
Spicy Pasta Salad with Feta and Basil Recipe 74
Spiral Pasta and Mixed Vegetable Salad Recipe 76
Easy Chicken Macaroni Salad Recipe 78
Cheesy Pasta Salad with Egg Recipe 79
Arugula and Pasta Salad with Pesto Sauce Recipe 80

PART 2 82

MEAT PASTA SAUCES 83

Awesome Sauce 84
Bobbies Spaghetti Sauce 86
Bolognese Meat Sauce in Instant Pot 88
Bolognese Sauce with Meat 90
Brians Favorite Sauce 92
Chef Johns Sunday Pasta Sauce 93
Chunky Red Sauce with Ground Italian Sausage 96
Classic Contadina Spaghetti Sauce 98
Contadina Quick Bolognese Sauce 99
Cubanelle and Veal Bolognese 100
Dads Spaghetti Sauce with Coffee 102
Divine Spaghetti Sauce 103
Easy Carbonara Sauce 105

EGGPLANT BOLOGNESE	106
ENHANCE THAT JAR OF SPAGHETTI SAUCE	109
GRANDMA AUGUSTAS SPAGHETTI SAUCE	110
GRANDMAS HOMEMADE ITALIAN SAUCE AND MEATBALLS	112
GRANDMAS MEAT SAUCE	114
GRANDMAS OLD ITALIAN SPAGHETTI SAUCE WITH MEATBALLS	115
HEARTY MEAT SAUCE	118
HOW TO MAKE BOLOGNESE SAUCE	119
ITALIAN MEAT SAUCE I	121
ITALIAN MEAT SAUCE II	123
ITALIAN SPAGHETTI SAUCE WITH MEATBALLS	126
ITALIAN TOMATO GRAVY	128
ITALIAN TOMATO SAUCE	130
JANSENS SPAGHETTI SAUCE AND MEATBALLS	132
JEANNES SLOW COOKER SPAGHETTI SAUCE	135
KAYS SPAGHETTI AND LASAGNA SAUCE	137
KICKED UP SAUSAGE MEAT SAUCE	139
LASAGNA FLATBREAD	141
LOTS OVEGGIES SAUSAGE SPAGHETTI SAUCE	143
MA HUNSICKERS SPAGHETTI SAUCE	144
MAMA PALOMBAS SPAGHETTI SAUCE	147
MARICAS SPAGHETTI MEAT SAUCE	149
MEAT GRAVY	150
MEATBALL SPAGHETTI SAUCE	153
MEATLOVERS SLOW COOKER SPAGHETTI SAUCE	155
MEATY SPAGHETTI SAUCE	157
MOMS QUICK PASTA SAUCE	158
MOMS SPAGHETTI SAUCE	160
MOMS SWEET SPAGHETTI SAUCE	161
NANAS SLOW COOKED MEATY TOMATO SAUCE	162
NORTH END SUNDAY GRAVY	164
NORTH ITALIAN MEAT SAUCE RAGU BOLOGNESE	167
NOT RED SPAGHETTI SAUCE	169
OLD FASHIONED SICILIAN SUCCO	170
OXTAIL RAGU	173
PAPAS TOMATO SAUCE	174

Pasta Sauce a la Pauly	176
Pasta Sauce with Italian Sausage	177
Pork and Shiitake Mushroom Ragu	179
ProscuittoShallot Vodka Sauce	181
Ragu Bologna Pasta Sauce	182
Restaurant Style Spaghetti Sauce	183
Ricks Tomato Gravy	184
Sams Original Sauce	186
Savory Italian Sausage Sauce	187
Sicilian Ragu	190
Slow Cooker Bolognese	191

Part 1

Introduction

This book offers a great collection of pasta recipes from traditional recipes to others that are exceptionally filling and rich in flavor.

Pasta is a staple food in Italy, but loved by many globally. This is because of its versatility as an ingredient, it can be used to create countless scrumptious dishes. From appetizers to mains... truly your options are endless. You can add fresh vegetables and herbs to make a salad just drizzle it with your choice of dressing such as balsamic vinaigrette or serve it with a sauce whether it is tomato based, cream-based, or the very popular pesto sauce.

Pasta makes a great alternative to rice and other starchy foods that gives us energy. It is very filling too that is why it can get you a long way without feeling hungry. So what are you waiting for? Go ahead and try one of these recipes on your next meal and surely your family and friends will be delighted!

Do's and Don'ts of Cooking the Perfect Pasta

Sometimes you might be wondering why your pasta turns out to be too mushy or that they stick together. Of course all of us wants to have a well-cooked pasta like what is usually served in Italian restaurants. The quality of a pasta that is cooked right is called "al dente" which means firm but tender in texture. How to achieve that? Read on for tips on how to cook and prepare that perfect pasta that you are yearning for.

1. Before cooking your store bought dried pasta, always check the package instructions. It will give you an idea on the correct cooking time of your pasta. In most cases 10-12 minutes is all you need to cook an al dente pasta. DO NOT OVER COOK or prolong cooking time than what is indicated in the package.
2. Use a large sized saucepan or stock pot when cooking your pasta, because when placed in boiling water and becomes cooked it will swell and double its size. Overcrowding might not give you your desired texture because it is not cooked properly. This will also result to pasta sticking at the bottom and sides of the pan and can clump together.
3. Have enough boiling water when cooking your pasta, this will prevent having tough and dry pasta. The basic rule is that for every pound of dry pasta you should use a gallon of boiling water.
4. To prevent pasta from sticking together a bit of olive oil can do the trick.
5. Adding some salt will not only enhance the taste of your pasta but it is also helpful in the cooking process as it will evenly distribute cooking and will increase boiling point.

6. Wait for the bubbles! Never add pasta if the water has not reach its boiling point. Otherwise your pasta will become mushy and undesirable texture.
7. Stirring your pasta from time to time will help prevent them from sticking together.
8. Take a bite on one pasta towards end of the cooking time. This will tell you if it is almost ready or not.
9. Once pasta is cooked, drain it using a colander. Shake it to remove excess water.
10. Store leftover pasta in a clean dry container with lid inside the refrigerator. But must use it for no longer than 3 days.
11. Save cooking time by using leftover pasta in your next meals. You can use them in making salads and soups.
12. Go economical! Save more by using leftover food with your pasta like roasted chicken, canned tuna, anchovies, roasted vegetables, and a lot more.

Anchovy Tomato and Mushroom Pasta Recipe

This pasta dish makes a hearty meal! The tomatoes and mushrooms blends nicely with the saltiness of the anchovies!

Preparation Time: 15 minutes
Total Time: 30 minutes
Yield: 2-3 servings

Ingredients
8 oz. spaghetti, dry
2 Tbsp. olive oil
3 garlic cloves, minced
1 medium red onion, chopped
2 medium ripe tomatoes, chopped
2 oz. anchovy fillets, bottled
1-2 tsp. dried chili flakes
1 cup button mushrooms, coarsely chopped
¼ cup fresh parsley, chopped
2 Tbsp. parmesan, grated
salt and pepper, to taste

Method
1. Cook pasta in a stockpot with boiling salted water for 12 minutes or until al dente (firm but tender). Drain. Set aside.
2. Heat oil in skillet over medium heat. Stir-fry garlic and onion until fragrant.
3. Add the tomatoes, anchovy fillets, and chilli flakes. Cook for 4-5 minutes. Crush the tomatoes using the back of the spoon. Add the mushrooms, stirring

occasionally for another 3 minutes. Season with salt and pepper to taste. Remove from heat.
4. Divide pasta into serving plates. Top with sauce and parsley. Sprinkle with parmesan.
5. Serve immediately and enjoy.

Arugula Pesto and Pine Nuts Pasta Recipe

Try this pasta recipe with arugula and pine nuts in Pesto sauce, so delicious!

Preparation Time: 15 minutes
Total Time: 30 minutes
Yield: 2-3 servings
Ingredients
8 oz. spaghetti noodles, dry
1 Tbsp. olive oil
3 garlic cloves, minced
1/3 cup oil-packed sun-dried tomatoes, drained and cut into strips
1/3 cup pesto sauce
1-2 tsp. dried chili flakes
handful arugula, chopped

2 Tbsp. pine nuts, toasted, to serve
salt and pepper, to taste
Method
1. Cook spaghetti in a stock pot of boiling salted water for 10-12 minutes. Drain. Set aside.
2. Heat oil in skillet over medium heat. Stir-fry garlic until fragrant.
3. Add the sun-dried tomatoes, pesto sauce, chilli flakes, and arugula. Cook for 4-5 minutes. Season with salt and pepper to taste.
4. Divide pasta into serving plates. Top with sauce. Sprinkle with pine nuts
5. Serve immediately and enjoy.
6. Enjoy.

Baked Macaroni with Turkey and Cheese Recipe

This baked macaroni recipe with roasted turkey and mozzarella is satisfyingly delicious!
Preparation Time: 15 minutes

Total Time: 45 minutes
Yield: 4-5 servings

Ingredients
1 lb. macaroni, dry
2 Tbsp. olive oil
3 garlic cloves, minced
1 medium onion, chopped
12 oz. roasted turkey breast, chopped
1 medium red bell pepper, chopped
1 cup tomato puree
1 tsp. paprika
2 Tbsp. fresh mixed herbs
½ cup mozzarella cheese, grated
fresh parsley, for garnish
salt and pepper, to taste

Method
1. Preheat oven at 180 C or 350 F.
2. Bring a large stock pot of salted water to a boil. Cook macaroni for 10-12 minutes. Drain. Set aside.
3. Heat oil in skillet over medium-high heat. Stir-fry garlic and onion until fragrant.
4. Add the turkey, bell pepper, tomato puree, paprika and mixed herbs. Cook for 5-7 minutes, stirring occasionally. Season with salt and pepper to taste.
5. Add the macaroni noodles and mix to coat with sauce. Transfer in a baking dish. Sprinkle with mozzarella cheese. Bake for 15-20 minutes. Remove from heat. Garnish with fresh parsley.
6. Serve immediately and enjoy.

Easy Beef and Zucchini Lasagna Recipe

This lovely pasta recipe with beef and zucchini is so delicious. Your family and friends will surely enjoy it!

Preparation Time: 20 minutes
Total Time: 50 minutes
Yield: 6 servings
Ingredients
1 lb. lasagna, dry
1 lb. zucchini, thinly sliced
1 lb. ground beef sirloin
2 Tbsp. olive oil
3 garlic cloves, minced
1 medium onion, chopped
1 ½ cup tomato puree
2 Tbsp. tomato paste
1 tsp. paprika
1 tsp. oregano, dried
2 Tbsp. fresh basil, chopped
½ cup mozzarella cheese, grated

fresh basil leaves, for garnish
salt and pepper, to taste

Method
1. Preheat oven at 180 C or 350 F.
2. Bring a large stock pot of salted water to a boil. Cook pasta for 10-12 minutes. Drain. Set aside.
3. Heat oil in skillet over medium-high heat. Stir-fry garlic and onion until fragrant.
4. Add the beef, stir-fry for 3-5 minutes or until browned.
5. Add the tomato puree, tomato paste, paprika, oregano, and basil. Cook for 5-6 minutes, stirring occasionally. Season with salt and pepper.
6. In a baking dish, make a layer of lasagna noodles, beef-tomato sauce, and sliced zucchini until everything is used up. Sprinkle with mozzarella cheese. Bake for about 20 minutes. Remove from heat. Garnish with fresh basil.
7. Serve immediately and enjoy.

Minced Turkey in Tomato Sauce with Herbs Recipe

You only need about 30 minutes to create this wonderful pasta dish with turkey, tomato sauce and herbs.

Preparation Time: 15 minutes
Total Time: 30 minutes
Yield: 6 servings
Ingredients
1 lb. spaghetti, dry
1 lb. turkey breast fillet, minced
2 Tbsp. olive oil
3 garlic cloves, minced
1 medium onion, chopped
1 ½ cup tomato sauce
2 Tbsp. tomato paste
1 tsp. oregano, dried
2 Tbsp. fresh basil, chopped
¼ cup parmesan cheese, grated
fresh basil leaves, for garnish
salt and pepper, to taste
Method
1. Bring a large stock pot of salted water to a boil. Cook pasta for 10-12 minutes. Drain. Set aside.
2. Meanwhile, heat oil in skillet over medium-high heat. Stir-fry garlic and onion until fragrant.
3. Add the turkey, stir-fry for 3-4 minutes or until browned.

4. Add the tomato sauce, tomato paste, oregano, and basil. Cook for 10-15 minutes, stirring occasionally. Season with salt and pepper. Remove from heat
5. Divide pasta in serving plates. Top with sauce. Sprinkle with parmesan. Garnish with fresh basil.
6. Serve immediately and enjoy.

Easy Pasta ala Vongole in White Wine Sauce Recipe

Want something extraordinary for dinner? Try this amazing pasta dish with clams in white wine sauce, you will surely love it!

Preparation Time: 15 minutes
Total Time: 35 minutes
Yield: 6 servings
Ingredients
1 lb. Angel hair pasta, dry
¼ cup butter

2 shallots, chopped
4 garlic cloves, crushed
2 ripe tomatoes, chopped
1 cup white wine
1 lb. vongole (clams), rinsed and drained
¼ cup continental parsley, chopped
¼ cup sweet basil, chopped
salt and pepper, to taste

Method
1. Cook the pasta in a large stock pot of boiling salted water, for about 10 minutes or until al dente. Drain. Set aside
2. Heat butter in a large saucepan over medium-high heat. Stir-fry onion and garlic until fragrant and onion softens.
3. Add the tomatoes, wine and clams. Cover with lid and cook for 5-7 minutes, stirring occasionally (discard unopened clams).
4. Add pasta and parsley, and basil. Toss gently to combine. Remove from heat. Season with salt and pepper. Transfer in a serving dish.
5. Serve immediately and enjoy.

Spaghetti with Meatball Sauce and Parmesan Recipe

This sumptuous pasta dish with meatball sauce is definitely worth trying!

Preparation Time: 20 minutes
Total Time: 45 minutes
Yield: 6 servings

Ingredients
1 lb. spaghetti, dry
1 lb. ground beef sirloin
2 Tbsp. fresh coriander, finely chopped
2 green onion, finely chopped
2 Tbsp. all-purpose flour
1 medium egg
2 Tbsp. olive oil
3 garlic cloves, minced
1 medium onion, chopped
1 cup Italian pasta sauce
1 cup tomato puree
1 tsp. paprika
1 tsp. oregano, dried

¼ cup parmesan cheese, grated
fresh basil leaves, for garnish
salt and pepper, to taste

Method
1. Bring a large stock pot of salted water to a boil. Cook pasta for 10-12 minutes. Drain. Set aside.
2. Meanwhile, place beef, coriander, green onion, flour, and egg in a large mixing bowl. Season with salt and pepper. Mix well. Form into small balls.
3. Heat oil in skillet over medium-high heat. Stir-fry garlic and onion until fragrant.
4. Add the meatballs, stir-fry for 3-4 minutes or until browned.
5. Add the Italian pasta sauce, tomato puree, paprika, and oregano. Reduce heat to low and cover with lid. Cook for 8-10 minutes, stirring occasionally. Season with salt and pepper. Remove from heat.
6. Divide pasta in individual plates. Top with meatball sauce. Sprinkle with parmesan cheese. Garnish with fresh basil.
7. Serve immediately and enjoy.

Spaghetti Carbonara with Roasted Turkey and Herbs Recipe

If you are craving for creamy pasta dish and got some leftover turkey, this is the
perfect recipe for you!
Preparation Time: 15 minutes
Total Time: 30 minutes
Yield: 6 servings

Ingredients
1 lb. spaghetti, dry
2 Tbsp. butter
3 garlic cloves, minced
1 medium onion, chopped
12 oz. roasted turkey breast fillet, coarsely chopped
¼ cup white wine
1 cup whole milk
½ cup all-purpose cream
½ tsp. oregano, dried
½ tsp. rosemary, dried

¼ cup parmesan cheese, grated
salt and pepper, to taste

Method
1. Bring a stock pot of salted water to a boil. Cook spaghetti for 10-12 minutes. Drain. Set aside.
2. Heat butter in saucepan over medium heat. Stir-fry garlic and onion until fragrant.
3. Add the turkey and white wine, cook for 2-3 minutes.
4. Add the milk, cream, oregano, and rosemary. Cook for 4-5 minutes, stirring frequently. Season with salt and pepper to taste.
5. Divide pasta in serving plates. Top with sauce. Sprinkle with parmesan.
6. Serve immediately and enjoy.

Spicy Spaghetti with Prawns and Herbs Recipe

This delightful pasta dish with prawns has a mild kick to it. Perfect for a quick family dinner!

Preparation Time: 15 minutes
Total Time: 30 minutes
Yield: 6 servings
Ingredients
1 lb. spaghetti, dry
1/3 cup butter
4 cloves garlic, minced
1 tsp. paprika
1 tsp. cumin, ground
1 lb. prawns, deveined, tails intact
1 tsp. dried sage
2 Tbsp. fresh parsley, chopped
½ cup sweet chili sauce
salt and pepper, to taste
Method

1. Cook spaghetti in a large saucepan of boiling water, as directed on the package. Drain. Set aside.
2. Heat oil in a skillet on medium-high heat. Stir-fry garlic, paprika, and cumin, until fragrant.
3. Add the prawns, sage, and parsley. Cook for 2-3 minutes, stirring occasionally. Stir in sweet-chili sauce. Season with salt and pepper.
4. Divide spaghetti in serving plates. Top with sauce. Garnish with parsley, if desired.
5. Serve immediately and enjoy.

Tagliatelle with Tuna in Pesto Sauce Recipe

This delectable pasta recipe with tuna in pesto sauce is so easy to prepare and healthy too!

Preparation Time: 15 minutes
Total Time: 30 minutes
Yield: 5-6 servings
Ingredients
1 lb. tagliatelle pasta
2 Tbsp. olive oil

1 medium brown onion, chopped
2 cloves garlic, minced
12 oz. canned tuna flakes, drained
¾ cup pesto sauce
¼ cup parmesan cheese, grated
½ cup continental parsley, chopped
salt and pepper, to taste

Method

1. Cook tagliatelle in a stock pot of boiling salted water until just tender, about 10-12 minutes. Drain. Set aside.
2. Meanwhile, heat oil in a large non-stick pan or skillet over medium heat. Stir-fry onion and garlic until fragrant.
3. Add tuna and pesto sauce. Cook, stirring for 2-3 minutes. Season with salt and pepper to taste.
4. Add pasta and toss to combine well. Transfer in serving plates.
5. Sprinkle with parmesan cheese and parsley.
6. Serve immediately and enjoy.

Spaghetti with Straw Mushroom and Spinach Recipe

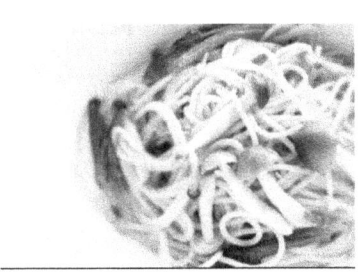

The vegetarian friendly pasta dish with straw mushrooms is great for a quick lunch or dinner when you don't have much time to prepare.

Preparation Time: 15 minutes
Total Time: 30 minutes
Yield: 6 servings

Ingredients
1 lb. spaghetti noodles, dry
¼ cup olive oil
1 medium brown onion, chopped
3 cloves garlic, minced
1 (15 oz.) can straw mushrooms, drained
4 cups baby spinach
½ cup white wine
¼ cup lemon juice
salt and pepper, to taste

Method
1. Bring a large stock pot of salted water to a boil. Cook spaghetti for 10-12 minutes. Drain. Set aside.

2. Heat oil in skillet over medium-high heat. Stir-fry onion and garlic until fragrant.
3. Add the mushrooms and white wine. Cook for 2-3 minutes, stirring occasionally.
4. Add the pasta, spinach and lemon juice, cook further 2-3 minutes. Season with salt and pepper. Transfer in individual plates.
5. Serve immediately and enjoy.

Creamy Mushroom Pasta with Paprika Recipe

This creamy pasta with mushroom and paprika is simply irresistible!
Preparation Time: 15 minutes
Total Time: 40 minutes
Yield: 2-3 servings
Ingredients
8 oz. tagliatelle, dry
2 Tbsp. butter
3 garlic cloves, minced
1 medium onion, chopped
2 tsp. paprika, divided

1 cup button mushrooms, thinly sliced
½ cup white wine
½ cup cream of mushroom, canned
½ cup whole milk
½ tsp. coriander seed, ground
¼ cup parmesan cheese, grated
fresh parsley, for garnish
salt and pepper, to taste

Method
1. Bring a stock pot of salted water to a boil. Cook tagliatelle for 10-12 minutes. Drain. Set aside.
2. Heat butter in saucepan over medium heat. Stir-fry garlic, onion, and 1 tsp. paprika until fragrant.
3. Add the mushrooms and white wine, stir-fry for 2 minutes.
4. Add the cream of mushroom, milk, and coriander. Cook for 4-5 minutes. . Season with salt and pepper to taste.
5. Add pasta and stir to combine. Transfer in a serving dish. Sprinkle with parmesan and remaining paprika. Garnish with fresh parsley.
6. Serve immediately and enjoy.

Baked Mac and Cheese Recipe

Even your kids can help you in making this awesome baked macaroni and cheese!
Preparation Time: 30 minutes
Total Time: 30 minutes
Yield: 6 servings

Ingredients
1 lb. macaroni, dry
2 Tbsp. plain flour
1 tsp. wholegrain mustard
1 cup evaporated milk
½ cup dried multigrain breadcrumbs
1 cup grated reduced-fat cheddar cheese
¼ cup mozzarella cheese, grated
Method
1. Preheat oven at 180 C or 350 F.
2. Bring a large stock pot of salted water to a boil. Cook macaroni for 10-12 minutes. Drain. Set aside.

3. Combine flour and mustard in a mixing bowl. Slowly pour evaporated milk, stirring constantly until dissolved completely.
4. Add pasta and stir to combine well. Transfer into a baking dish. Top with mozzarella and sprinkle with breadcrumbs. Bake for 15-20 minutes or until golden.
5. Serve and enjoy.

Baked Ziti with Meat in Tomato Sauce Recipe

Indulge in this delightful baked pasta with meat in tomato sauce.

Preparation Time: 20 minutes
Total Time: 40 minutes
Yield: 6 servings
Ingredients
1 lb. ziti, dry
1 lb. beef sirloin, ground
2 Tbsp. olive oil
3 garlic cloves, minced

1 medium onion, chopped
1 ½ cup tomato sauce
2 Tbsp. tomato paste
1 tsp. oregano, dried
2 Tbsp. fresh basil, chopped
½ cup mozzarella cheese, grated
salt and pepper, to taste

Method
1. Preheat oven at 180 C or 350 F.
2. Bring a large stock pot of salted water to a boil. Cook ziti for 10-12 minutes. Drain. Set aside.
3. Heat oil in a large skillet over medium-high heat. Stir-fry garlic and onion until fragrant.
4. Add the beef, stir-fry for 3-4 minutes or until browned.
5. Add the tomato sauce, tomato paste, oregano, and basil. Cook for 5-6 minutes, stirring occasionally. Season with salt and pepper.
6. Add pasta and stir to combine well. Transfer in a baking dish and sprinkle with mozzarella cheese. Bake for 15-20 minutes. Remove from heat.
7. Serve immediately and enjoy.

Creamy Pasta with Zucchini and Mushroom Recipe

Hosting a dinner party? Impress your guests with this scrumptious pasta with zucchini and mushroom.

Preparation Time: 15 minutes
Total Time: 45 minutes
Yield: 4 servings
Ingredients
8 oz. spaghetti, dry
2 Tbsp. butter
3 garlic cloves, minced
1 medium onion, chopped
1 cup button mushrooms, sliced
1 medium zucchini, sliced
¼ cup white wine
½ cup all-purpose cream
½ cup whole milk
½ tsp. oregano, dried
½ tsp. coriander seed, ground

¼ cup parmesan cheese, grated
salt and pepper, to taste

Method
1. Bring a stock pot of salted water to a boil. Cook spaghetti for 10-12 minutes. Drain. Set aside.
2. Heat butter in saucepan over medium heat. Stir-fry garlic and onion until fragrant.
3. Add the mushrooms, zucchini, and white wine, stir-fry for 2-3 minutes.
4. Add the cream, milk, oregano and coriander. Cook for 4-5 minutes, stirring frequently. Season with salt and pepper to taste.
5. Add pasta and stir to combine. Transfer in a serving dish. Sprinkle with parmesan.
6. Serve immediately and enjoy.

Fettuccini with Shrimp Lemon and Parsley Recipe

This easy to cook fettuccini dish features shrimps, garlic, lemon, and parsley.

Preparation Time: 30 minutes
Total Time: 30 minutes
Yield: 5-6 servings
Ingredients
1 lb. fettuccini, dry
¼ cup olive oil
4 cloves garlic, minced
12 oz. shrimps, deveined, tails intact
2 tsp. dill, chopped
2 Tbsp. fresh parsley, chopped
¼ cup lemon juice
salt and pepper, to taste
Method
1. Cook fettuccini in a large saucepan of boiling water, as directed on the package. Drain. Return to pan and cover to keep warm.
2. Heat oil in a skillet on medium-high heat. Stir-fry garlic until fragrant.
3. Add the shrimps, dill, and parsley. Cook for 3-5 minutes, stirring occasionally. Stir in lemon juice. Season with salt and pepper.
4. Add fettuccini and toss to combine. Cook further 2-3 minutes. Transfer in individual plates. Garnish with parsley, if desired.
5. Serve and enjoy.

Italian Seafood Pasta Recipe

This scrumptious pasta recipe combines the flavors tomatoes, herbs and the sea.

Preparation Time: 15 minutes
Total Time: 35 minutes
Yield: 6 servings
Ingredients
1 lb. tagliatelle noodles, dry
2 Tbsp. olive oil
1 medium brown onion, chopped
2 cloves garlic, minced
½ cup white wine
1 cup Italian pasta sauce
1 lb. fresh seafood marinara mix
½ cup flat-leaf parsley, chopped
Method

1. Cook tagliatelle in a stock pot with boiling salted water, according to package directions. Drain. Set aside.
2. Heat oil in a large saucepan over medium heat. Stir-fry onion and garlic until fragrant. Stir in wine and cook for 1-2 minutes.
3. Add the Italian pasta sauce. Bring to the boil, stirring occasionally.
4. Add marinara mix and stir to combine well. Cook over medium heat for 3-4 minutes or until just cooked.
5. Stir in parsley. Season with salt and pepper to taste.
6. Divide cooked tagliatelle in serving plates. Top with marinara sauce.
7. Serve and enjoy.

Pasta Salmon and Cheese Casserole Recipe

This sensational homemade pasta dish makes a filling meal for lunch or dinner!
Preparation Time: 20 minutes
Total Time: 45 minutes
Yield: 6 servings
Ingredients
1 lb. macaroni, dry
2 Tbsp. olive oil
3 garlic cloves, minced
1 medium onion, chopped
12 oz. baked pink salmon, cut into small pieces
1 medium red bell pepper, chopped
1 cup tomato sauce
1 tsp. paprika
2 Tbsp. fresh basil
¼ cup cheddar cheese, grated
¼ cup mozzarella cheese, grated
fresh basil or parsley, for garnish
salt and pepper, to taste
Method

1. Preheat oven at 180 C or 350 F.
2. Bring a large stock pot of salted water to a boil. Cook macaroni for 10-12 minutes. Drain. Set aside.
3. Heat oil in skillet over medium-high heat. Stir-fry garlic and onion until fragrant.
4. Add the salmon, bell pepper, tomato sauce, paprika and basil. Cook for 4-5 minutes, stirring occasionally. Season with salt and pepper to taste.
5. Add the macaroni noodles and mix to coat with sauce. Transfer in a baking dish. Sprinkle with cheddar and mozzarella cheese. Bake for 15-20 minutes. Remove from heat. Garnish with fresh basil or parsley.
6. Serve immediately and enjoy.

Penne with Minced Meat in Tomato Sauce Recipe

This wonderful pasta recipe has a great blend of flavors from the beef, tomato and herbs.

Preparation Time: 15 minutes
Total Time: 35 minutes
Yield: 6 servings

Ingredients

1 lb. penne, dry
2 Tbsp. olive oil
3 garlic cloves, minced
1 medium onion, chopped
1 lb. beef sirloin, minced
1 cup tomato sauce
2 Tbsp. tomato paste
½ tsp. dried sage
½ tsp. dried thyme
¼ cup parmesan cheese, grated
fresh basil, for garnish
salt and pepper, to taste

Method

1. Cook penne in a stockpot of boiling salted water, as directed in the package. Drain. Set aside.
2. Heat oil in saucepan over medium-high heat. Stir-fry garlic and onion until fragrant.
3. Add the beef and cook until browned, about 3-4 minutes.
4. Add the tomato sauce, tomato paste, sage, and thyme. Cook for 5-6 minutes, stirring occasionally. Season with salt and pepper to taste. Remove from heat.
5. Divide pasta in serving plates. Top with sauce. Sprinkle with parmesan. Garnish with basil.

6. Serve immediately and enjoy.

Fettuccini with Creamy Mushroom Sauce Recipe

This fettuccini dish with creamy mushroom sauce is a great way to treat yourself after a long busy day.

Preparation Time: 15 minutes
Total Time: 30 minutes
Yield: 4-5 servings
Ingredients
1 lb. fettuccini noodles, dry
2 Tbsp. butter
3 garlic cloves, minced
1 medium onion, chopped
1 cup button mushrooms, chopped
¼ cup white wine
½ cup cream of mushroom, canned
½ cup whole milk

2 Tbsp. heavy cream
½ tsp. dried parsley
½ tsp. dried oregano
¼ cup parmesan cheese, grated
fresh parsley, for garnish
salt and pepper, to taste

Method

1. Bring a large stock pot of salted water to a boil. Cook fettuccini for 10-12 minutes. Drain. Set aside.
2. Heat butter in large saucepan over medium heat. Stir-fry garlic and onion until fragrant.
3. Add the mushrooms and white wine, cook for 2 minutes.
4. Add the cream of mushroom, milk, cream, and dried herbs. Cook for 5-6 minutes. Season with salt and pepper to taste.
5. Add pasta and stir to combine. Transfer in a serving dish. Sprinkle with parmesan. Garnish with fresh parsley.
6. Serve immediately and enjoy.

Fusilli with Salmon and Spinach in Cream Sauce Recipe

This quick and easy one-dish meal recipe with pasta, salmon, and spinach taste really good!
Preparation Time: 30 minutes
Total Time: 30 minutes
Yield: 4 servings
Ingredients
1 lb. fusilli (spiral pasta), dry
2 Tbsp. butter
4 cloves garlic, minced
8 oz. baked salmon, flaked
¼ cup white wine
1 cup all-purpose cream
4 cups baby spinach
1 Tbsp. dill, chopped
2 Tbsp. lemon zest, finely grated
Method

1. Cook fusilli in a large saucepan of boiling water, as directed on the package. Drain. Return to pan. Set aside.
2. Heat butter in a skillet on medium heat. Stir-fry garlic until fragrant.
3. Add the salmon and wine. Cook for 1-2 minutes, stirring occasionally. Stir in cream, spinach, and dill. Cook further 3-4 minutes. Season with salt and pepper.
4. Add fusilli and toss to combine. Cook for another 2-3 minutes. Transfer in individual plates. Garnish with parsley, if desired.
5. Serve and enjoy.

Herbed Artichoke Pasta with Parmesan Recipe

The artichoke, herbs, and parmesan gives a lovely flavor to this wonderful pasta dish.
Preparation Time: 20 minutes
Total Time: 20 minutes
Yield: 4 servings

Ingredients

4 cups penne, cooked

1 cup marinated artichoke hearts, drained and cut into small pieces

¼ cup parmesan, grated

fresh basil, for garnish

salt and pepper, to taste

Lemon Vinaigrette with Basil Dressing:

½ cup extra-virgin olive oil

2 Tbsp. lemon juice

1 Tbsp. lemon zest

1 tsp. basil, dried

Method

1. Whisk together oil, lemon juice, lemon zest, and basil in a small glass bowl. Set aside.
2. Combine penne and artichokes in a large salad bowl. Drizzle with dressing. Season with salt and pepper. Toss to coat.
3. Transfer in individual plates. Sprinkle with parmesan and garnish with fresh basil.
4. Serve and enjoy.

Creamy Mac and Cheese Recipe

If you love mac and cheese, try this super creamy and cheesy version!

Preparation Time: 10 minutes
Total Time: 25 minutes
Yield: 6 servings

Ingredients
1 lb. macaroni, dry
2 Tbsp. butter
2 Tbsp. all-purpose flour
1 cup evaporated milk
1 cup cheddar cheese, grated

Method
1. Bring a large stock pot of salted water to a boil. Cook macaroni for 10-12 minutes. Drain. Set aside.
2. Heat butter in a small saucepan over medium heat. Stir in flour cook for 20 seconds.
3. Slowly pour evaporated milk, stirring constantly. Cook for 2 minutes or until thickened.
4. Add cheddar cheese, stir to combine well. Cook further 1 minute or until melted.
5. Place cooked macaroni in a large bowl. Pour cheese sauce mixture. Toss to coat.
6. Serve and enjoy.

Chicken Lasagna with Bechamel Sauce Recipe

This is a great alternative to your regular meat pasta!

Preparation Time: 25 minutes
Total Time: 45 minutes
Yield: 6 servings
Ingredients
1 lb. lasagna, dry
1 lb. chicken breast fillet, ground
2 Tbsp. olive oil
3 garlic cloves, minced
1 medium onion, chopped
1 ½ cup Italian pasta sauce
2 Tbsp. tomato paste
1 tsp. paprika
2 Tbsp. fresh basil, chopped
2 Tbsp. fresh parsley, chopped
½ cup mozzarella cheese, grated
fresh basil, for garnish
salt and pepper, to taste

Bechamel Sauce:
1 Tbsp. butter
2 Tbsp. all-purpose flour
1 can evaporated milk
½ cup cheddar cheese
2 Tbsp. parmesan cheese
½ tsp. nutmeg

Method

1. **To Prepare the Bechamel Sauce:** Heat butter in a saucepan over medium heat. Stir in flour and cook for 15-20 seconds. Add the milk gradually and cook for 3-5 minutes, stirring until thickened. Add cheddar, parmesan, and nutmeg. Cook further 1-2 minutes. Remove from heat.
2. Preheat oven at 180 C or 350 F.
3. Bring a large stock pot of salted water to a boil. Cook pasta for 10-12 minutes. Drain. Set aside.
4. Heat oil in skillet over medium-high heat. Stir-fry garlic and onion until fragrant.
5. Add the chicken, stir-fry for 3-4 minutes or until browned.
6. Add the Italian pasta sauce, tomato paste, paprika, basil, and parsley. Cook for 5-6 minutes, stirring occasionally. Season with salt and pepper.
7. In a baking dish, make a layer of lasagna noodles, chicken sauce, and bechamel sauce until everything is used up. Sprinkle with mozzarella cheese. Bake for 15-20 minutes. Remove from heat. Garnish with fresh basil.

8. Serve immediately and enjoy.

Pasta with Alfredo Sauce Recipe

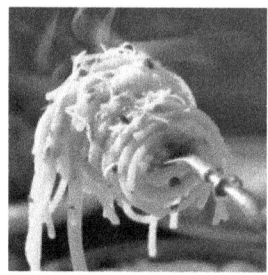

Enjoy this healthy version of a traditional pasta dish in milk-based sauce with herbs!
Preparation Time: 15 minutes
Total Time: 30 minutes
Yield: 4-5 servings
Ingredients
1 lb. spaghetti, dry
2 Tbsp. butter
3 cloves garlic, crushed
1 medium onion, chopped
1 tsp. fresh thyme leaves
2 Tbsp. all-purpose flour
2 cups whole milk
¼ cup grated parmesan cheese
salt and pepper, to taste
fresh parsley, to serve
Method
1. Bring a large stock pot of salted water to a boil. Cook spaghetti for 10-12 minutes. Drain. Set aside.

2. Heat butter in saucepan over medium heat. Stir-fry garlic and onion until fragrant. Stir in flour until combined.
3. Slowly pour milk while stirring constantly. Cook until thickened about 3-5 minutes. Season with salt and pepper to taste.
4. Add pasta and thyme. Stir to combine. Transfer in a serving dish. Sprinkle with parmesan. Garnish with fresh thyme.
5. Serve immediately and enjoy.

Seafood Pasta with Fresh Parmesan Recipe

This seafood pasta recipe is so good, perfect for a quick lunch or dinner.

Preparation Time: 15 minutes
Total Time: 35 minutes
Yield: 6 servings
Ingredients
1 lb. dried fettuccini
2 Tbsp. olive oil

2 shallots, chopped
4 garlic cloves, crushed
2 ripe tomatoes, seeded, finely chopped
1 cup dry white wine
1 lb. fresh marinara mix
2 Tbsp. lemon juice
2 Tbsp. fresh mixed herbs
¼ cup fresh parmesan, grated
salt and pepper, to taste

Method
1. Cook the pasta in a large stock pot of boiling salted water, for about 10-12 minutes or until al dente. Drain. Set aside
2. Heat oil in a large saucepan over medium-high heat. Stir-fry onion and garlic until fragrant and onion softens.
3. Add the tomatoes, wine and marinara mix. Cover with lid and cook for 5-7 minutes, stirring occasionally.
4. Add cooked fettuccini, lemon juice, and herbs. Toss gently to combine. Remove from heat. Season with salt and pepper. Transfer in a serving dish. Sprinkle with parmesan.
5. Serve immediately and enjoy.

Pasta with Mixed Vegetables Stir Fry Recipe

This healthy recipe makes a great lunch, the vegetables and herbs compliments
well with the pasta.
Preparation Time: 15 minutes
Total Time: 30 minutes
Yield: 2-3 servings
Ingredients
2 cups rotini pasta, cooked
2 Tbsp. olive oil
3 cloves garlic, sliced
1 cup broccoli florets
1 medium carrot, cut into strips
1 medium red bell pepper, cut into strips
1 tsp. coriander seed, ground
1 Tbsp. fresh coriander, finely chopped
¼ cup lemon juice
salt and pepper, to taste
Method
1. Heat oil in a skillet over medium-high heat. Stir-fry garlic and onion until fragrant.

2. Add broccoli, carrot, and pepper. Cook for 5-7 minutes or until crisp-tender.
3. Add pasta, lemon juice, coriander seed, and fresh coriander. Cook, stirring further 2-3 minutes. Season with salt and pepper to taste. Transfer in a serving dish.
4. Serve and enjoy.

Pasta with Sun-Dried Tomatoes and Anchovies Recipe

If you are looking for a delicious meal to serve your family, this is the recipe for you!
Preparation Time: 15 minutes
Total Time: 30 minutes
Yield: 4-5 servings
Ingredients
1 lb. rigatoni or penne pasta, dry
2 Tbsp. olive oil
3 garlic cloves, minced
1 medium onion, chopped

3 oz. bottled anchovies, drained
½ cup sun-dried tomato in oil, drained and chopped
1 cup tomato puree
½ tsp. dried basil
½ tsp. dried oregano
¼ cup parmesan cheese, grated
fresh basil, for garnish
salt and pepper, to taste

Method
1. Bring a large stock pot of salted water to a boil. Cook pasta for 10-12 minutes. Drain. Set aside.
2. Heat oil in skillet over medium-high heat. Stir-fry garlic and onion until fragrant.
3. Add the anchovies, sun-dried tomatoes, tomato puree, and herbs. Cook for 5-7 minutes, stirring frequently.
4. Add the pasta and mix to coat with sauce. Season with salt and pepper to taste. Remove from heat. Transfer in a serving dish. Sprinkle with parmesan cheese. Garnish with fresh basil.
5. Serve immediately and enjoy.

Penne with Chicken in White Sauce Recipe

A delightful pasta recipe that is high in protein and can be enjoyed either lunch or dinner.

Preparation Time: 15 minutes
Total Time: 30 minutes
Yield: 2-3 servings

Ingredients
8 oz. penne, dry
2 Tbsp. butter
3 garlic cloves, minced
1 medium onion, chopped
8 oz. roasted chicken breast, shredded
¼ cup white wine
2/3 cup all-purpose cream
2/3 cup whole milk
½ tsp. Italian seasoning
¼ cup parmesan cheese, grated
fresh parsley, for garnish

salt and pepper, to taste

Method
1. Cook penne in a stock pot of boiling salted water for 10-12 minutes. Drain. Set aside.
2. Heat butter in saucepan over medium heat. Stir-fry garlic, onion until fragrant.
3. Add the chicken and white wine, cook for 2 minutes.
4. Add the cream, milk, and Italian seasoning. Cook further 5-7 minutes. Season with salt and pepper to taste.
5. Divide pasta in serving plates. Top with sauce. Sprinkle with parmesan. Garnish with fresh parsley.
6. Serve immediately and enjoy.

Penne with Eggplant Tomato and Basil Recipe

Try this humble yet delicious pasta recipe with eggplant, tomato and basil for a satisfying lunch!

Preparation Time: 15 minutes
Total Time: 30 minutes
Yield: 4-5 servings
Ingredients
1 lb. penne, dry
2 Tbsp. olive oil
3 garlic cloves, minced
1 medium onion, chopped
2 medium ripe tomatoes, chopped
2 medium eggplant, diced
1 cup tomato puree
1 tsp. paprika
2 Tbsp. fresh basil, chopped
½ cup feta cheese, crumbled
fresh basil, for garnish
salt and pepper, to taste

Method
1. Bring a large stock pot of salted water to a boil. Cook penne for 10-12 minutes. Drain. Set aside.
2. Heat oil in skillet over medium-high heat. Stir-fry garlic, onion, and tomatoes until fragrant.
3. Add the eggplant, tomato puree, paprika and basil. Reduce heat and cook for 10 minutes or until eggplant is tender, stirring occasionally. Season with salt and pepper to taste. Remove from heat.
4. Divide pasta in individual plates. Top with sauce. Sprinkle with crumbled feta cheese. Garnish with fresh basil.
5. Serve immediately and enjoy.

Spaghetti with Meat and Veggies in Tomato Sauce Recipe

Easy and delicious pasta with meat and vegetables in tomato sauce.

Preparation Time: 15 minutes

Total Time: 30 minutes
Yield: 6 servings

Ingredients

1 lb. spaghetti, dry
2 Tbsp. olive oil
3 garlic cloves, minced
1 medium onion, chopped
2 medium ripe tomatoes, chopped
1 lb. beef sirloin, ground
1 medium red bell pepper, chopped
1 medium carrot, chopped
1 cup tomato puree
½ tsp. dried oregano
½ tsp. dried thyme
¼ cup parmesan cheese, grated
fresh parsley, for garnish
salt and pepper, to taste

Method

1. Bring a large stock pot of salted water to a boil. Cook spaghetti for 10-12 minutes. Drain. Set aside.
2. Heat oil in skillet over medium-high heat. Stir-fry garlic, onion, and tomatoes until fragrant.
3. Add the beef and cook until browned, about 3-4 minutes.
4. Add the bell pepper, carrot, tomato puree, oregano, and thyme. Cook for 10-15 minutes, stirring occasionally. Season with salt and pepper to taste. Remove from heat.
5. Divide pasta in serving plates. Top with sauce. Sprinkle with parmesan. Garnish with parsley.

6. Serve immediately and enjoy.

Spaghetti in Pesto Sauce with Parmesan Recipe

This classic Italian pasta recipe with pesto and parmesan is best served for lunch or light dinner.

Preparation Time: 15 minutes
Total Time: 30 minutes
Yield: 4-5 servings
Ingredients
1 lb. spaghetti, dry

Basil Pesto Sauce with Pine Nuts:
2 cloves garlic
2 cups fresh basil leaves, loosely packed
2 Tbsp. pine nuts
¼ cup parmesan, grated
¼ cup extra-virgin olive oil
Method

1. Place garlic, basil, pine nuts and parmesan in a food processor. Process until smooth, scraping down sides from time to time. With motor running, gradually add the oil. Continue to process until well combined. Transfer to a bowl. Stir in parmesan and season with salt and pepper to taste. Set aside.
2. Cook spaghetti in a large saucepan with boiling water, following the package instructions. Drain. Return pasta to saucepan.
3. Add the pesto sauce and toss to coat. Transfer in a serving dish. Garnish with fresh basil and sprinkle some pine nuts, if desired
4. Serve and enjoy.

Cumin Spiced Spaghetti Puttanesca Recipe

The spices give a nice flavor to this traditional Italian pasta recipe.
Preparation Time: 30 minutes
Total Time: 30 minutes
Yield: 6 servings
Ingredients
1 lb. spaghetti, dry

¼ cup olive oil
3 cloves garlic, minced
1 medium onion, sliced
3 medium tomatoes, diced
2 Tbsp. capers, drained
¼ cup olives, drained, sliced
½ tsp. chili powder
½ tsp. coriander, ground
1 tsp. cumin, ground
¼ cup lemon juice
salt and pepper, to taste
fresh parsley, for garnish

Method

1. Cook spaghetti in a large saucepan of boiling salted water, as directed on the package. Drain. Set aside.
2. Heat oil in a skillet on medium-high heat. Stir-fry garlic and onion until fragrant.
3. Add tomatoes, capers, olives, chili, coriander, and cumin. Cook for 3-5 minutes, stirring frequently. Stir in lemon juice. Season with salt and pepper.
4. Divide pasta in individual plates. Top with puttanesca sauce. Garnish with parsley, if desired.
5. Serve and enjoy.

Spaghetti with Asparagus and Cherry Tomatoes Recipe

Try this pasta recipe for a tasty, easy, and satisfying meal in minutes!

Preparation Time: 30 minutes
Total Time: 30 minutes
Yield: 5-6 servings

Ingredients
1 lb. spaghetti, dry
¼ cup olive oil
3 cloves garlic, minced
1 bunch asparagus, trimmed and cut into small pieces
1 cup cherry tomatoes, halved
2 tsp. dill, chopped
2 Tbsp. fresh basil, chopped
¼ cup balsamic vinegar
salt and pepper, to taste
fresh basil, to serve

Method

1. Cook spaghetti in a large saucepan of boiling salted water, as directed on the package. Drain. Set aside.
2. Heat oil in a large skillet on medium-high heat. Stir-fry garlic until fragrant.
3. Add the asparagus, cherry tomatoes, dill, and basil. Cook for about 7-10 minutes or until tender, stirring occasionally. Stir in balsamic vinegar. Season with salt and pepper.
4. Add spaghetti and toss to combine. Cook further 3-4 minutes. Transfer in individual plates. Garnish with basil, if desired.
5. Serve and enjoy.

Spaghetti with Stewed Tomatoes Basil and Garlic Recipe

This is a very easy recipe that is packed with flavor and can make your tummy happy!
Preparation Time: 30 minutes
Total Time: 30 minutes
Yield: 5-6 servings

Ingredients
1 lb. spaghetti, dry
2 Tbsp. olive oil
4 cloves garlic, minced
2 cups stewed tomatoes, sliced
½ cup white wine
¼ cup fresh basil, chopped
¼ cup parmesan cheese, grated
salt and pepper, to taste
fresh basil, for garnish

Method
1. Bring a stock pot of salted water to a boil. Cook spaghetti for 10-12 minutes. Drain. Set aside.
2. Heat oil in a large saucepan over medium heat. Stir-fry garlic until fragrant.
3. Add the stewed tomatoes, white wine, and basil. Cook for 5 minutes, stirring frequently. Season with salt and pepper to taste.
4. Add pasta and stir to combine. Transfer in a serving dish. Sprinkle with parmesan. Garnish with fresh basil.
5. Serve immediately and enjoy.

Veggie and Pasta Medley Recipe

This vegan-friendly pasta recipe with vegetables makes a great one-dish meal is you are watching your weight.
Preparation Time: 15 minutes
Total Time: 30 minutes
Yield: 4-5 servings
Ingredients
1 lb. penne, dry
2 Tbsp. olive oil
3 cloves garlic, minced
2 cups broccoli florets
1 medium carrot, thinly sliced
2 medium celery stalks, thinly sliced
1 tsp. coriander seed, ground
2 Tbsp. fresh parsley, chopped
¼ cup lemon juice
salt and pepper, to taste
Method
1. Bring a stock pot of salted water to a boil. Cook penne for 10-12 minutes. Drain. Set aside.

2. Heat oil in a large saucepan over medium heat. Stir-fry garlic until fragrant.
3. Add the broccoli, carrot, celery, coriander, and parsley. Cook for 7-10 minutes or until crisp-tender, stirring occasionally.
4. Add pasta and lemon juice. Toss to combine well. Season with salt and pepper to taste. Transfer in a serving dish.
5. Serve immediately and enjoy.

Tagliatelle with Spinach Pesto and Peas Recipe

This pasta dish is a 100% crowd-pleaser because of its rich in flavor and very filling.
Preparation Time: 15 minutes
Total Time: 30 minutes
Yield: 6 servings
Ingredients
1 lb. tagliatelle pasta
2 Tbsp. olive oil
1 medium brown onion, chopped
2 cloves garlic, minced

1 cup baby spinach, chopped
1 cup green peas
¾ cup pesto sauce
¼ cup parmesan cheese, grated
salt and pepper, to taste

Method
1. Cook tagliatelle in a stock pot of boiling salted water until just tender, about 10-12 minutes. Drain. Set aside.
2. Meanwhile, heat oil in a large non-stick pan or skillet over medium heat. Stir-fry onion and garlic until fragrant.
3. Add spinach, peas, and pesto sauce. Cook, stirring for 2-3 minutes. Season with salt and pepper to taste.
4. Add pasta and toss to combine well. Transfer in serving plates.
5. Sprinkle with parmesan cheese.
6. Serve immediately and enjoy.

Tagliatelle with Seafood in Tomato Sauce Recipe

This mouthwatering pasta dish with seafood in tomato sauce makes a nice treat after a long day at work.

Preparation Time: 15 minutes
Total Time: 35 minutes
Yield: 6 servings

Ingredients

1 lb. tagliatelle pasta
¼ cup olive oil
1 medium onion, chopped
3 cloves garlic, minced
2 medium ripe tomatoes
½ cup white wine
½ cup tomato sauce
2 Tbsp. tomato paste
1 lb. fresh seafood marinara mix
½ tsp. dried sage
½ tsp. dried thyme
salt and pepper, to taste

Method

1. Bring large stock pot of salted water to a boil. Cook pasta for 10-12 minutes. Drain. Set aside.
2. Meanwhile, heat oil in a large frying pan over medium heat. Stir-fry onion and garlic until fragrant.
3. Add tomatoes, wine, tomato sauce, and tomato paste. Cook for 3-5 minutes, stirring frequently.
4. Add the marinara mix, sage, and thyme. Cook further 5 minutes or until cooked through. Season with salt and pepper. Remove from heat.

5. Divide pasta in serving plates. Top with marinara sauce.
6. Serve immediately and enjoy.

Spaghetti with Meat and Mushroom Recipe

Pasta lovers will surely enjoy this delicious pasta dish with beef and mushrooms in Italian sauce.

Preparation Time: 20 minutes
Total Time: 30 minutes
Yield: 6 servings
Ingredients
1 lb. spaghetti, dry
2 Tbsp. olive oil
3 garlic cloves, minced
1 medium onion, chopped
1 lb. ground beef sirloin
1 cup button mushrooms, coarsely chopped
2 cups Italian pasta sauce
1 tsp. paprika
fresh basil leaves, for garnish

salt and pepper, to taste

parmesan cheese, to serve

Method

1. Bring a large stock pot of salted water to a boil. Cook pasta for 10-12 minutes. Drain. Set aside.
2. Heat oil in skillet over medium-high heat. Stir-fry garlic and onion until fragrant.
3. Add beef, stir-fry for 3-4 minutes or until browned.
4. Add mushrooms, Italian pasta sauce, and paprika. Cook for 7-10 minutes, stirring occasionally. Season with salt and pepper. Remove from heat.
5. Divide cooked spaghetti in individual plates. Top with sauce. Garnish with fresh basil.
6. Serve with parmesan cheese if desired and enjoy.

Roasted Chicken Vegetable and Pasta Salad

This awesome pasta recipe with roasted chicken, and vegetables is very filling and yummy!
Preparation Time: 20 minutes
Total Time: 20 minutes
Yield: 4-5 servings
Ingredients
8 oz. roasted chicken breast, cut into strips
4 cups baby spinach
2 cups shell pasta, cooked
1 cup roasted vegetables, cut into small pieces
¼ cup parmesan cheese, grated
Lemon Vinaigrette Dressing:
½ cup extra-virgin olive oil
2 Tbsp. lemon juice
1 tsp. lemon rind, finely grated
½ tsp. thyme, dried
salt and pepper, to taste
Method
1. Whisk together oil, lemon juice, lemon zest, and thyme in a small glass bowl. Set aside

2. Combine chicken, spinach, pasta, and vegetables in a large salad bowl. Drizzle with dressing. Season with salt and pepper. Toss to coat.
3. Transfer in individual plates. Sprinkle with parmesan.
4. Serve and enjoy.

Easy Macaroni and Vegetable Salad Recipe

Need something quick, easy, and satisfying recipe for lunch? This is the perfect recipe for you!
Preparation Time: 20 minutes
Total Time: 20 minutes
Yield: 4 servings
Ingredients
2 cups macaroni, cooked
1 cup cherry tomatoes, halved
1 cup broccoli florets, cooked
1 cup baby carrots
Balsamic Vinaigrette Dressing:
½ cup extra-virgin olive oil
2 Tbsp. balsamic vinegar

1 Tbsp. honey
½ tsp. basil, dried
salt and pepper, to taste
Method
1. Whisk together oil, balsamic vinegar, honey, and basil in a small glass bowl. Set aside
2. Combine macaroni, cherry tomatoes, broccoli, and baby carrots in a large salad bowl. Drizzle with dressing. Season with salt and pepper. Toss to coat.
3. Transfer in individual plates.
4. Serve and enjoy.

Tuna Pasta Salad Recipe with Yogurt-Herb Dressing

This wonderful tuna pasta salad recipe is great for lunch or light dinner!
Preparation Time: 20 minutes
Total Time: 20 minutes
Yield: 2-3 servings
Ingredients

2 cups rigati or penne pasta, cooked
8 oz. tuna flakes in oil, canned, drained
1 medium red bell pepper, cut into strips
2 medium celery stalks, thinly sliced
¼ cup fresh parsley, chopped
Yogurt-Herb Dressing:
½ cup Greek yogurt
2 Tbsp. lemon juice
½ tsp. basil, dried
salt and pepper, to taste

Method
1. Whisk together yogurt, lemon juice, and basil in a small glass bowl. Set aside.
2. Combine macaroni, tuna bell pepper, and celery in a large salad bowl. Season with salt and pepper. Toss to combine well.
3. Transfer in individual plates. Drizzle with yogurt-herb dressing. Sprinkle with fresh parsley.
4. Serve and enjoy.

Pasta with Feta Tomato and Pepper Recipe

Need some lunch ideas? Why not try this one, it's tasty, easy, and healthy too!

Preparation Time: 20 minutes
Total Time: 20 minutes
Yield: 2-3 servings

Ingredients
2 cups ribbon pasta, cooked
1 cup cherry tomatoes, halved
1 medium yellow bell pepper, chopped
6 oz. feta cheese, diced
2 Tbsp. fresh parsley, chopped
salt and pepper, to taste

Balsamic Vinaigrette Dressing:
¼ cup extra-virgin olive oil
2 Tbsp. balsamic vinegar
1 Tbsp. honey
½ tsp. basil, dried

Method

1. Mix together oil, balsamic vinegar, honey, and basil in a small glass bowl. Set aside.
2. Combine pasta, cherry tomatoes, bell pepper, and feta cheese in a large salad bowl. Drizzle with dressing. Season with salt and pepper. Toss to coat.
3. Transfer in individual plates.

4. Serve and enjoy.

Spaghetti with Tomato Feta and Olives Recipe

This fresh and delightful pasta and veggie salad is ready in less than 30 minutes!
Preparation Time: 10 minutes
Total Time: 20 minutes
Yield: 2-3 servings
Ingredients
2 cups spaghetti, cooked
1 cup grape tomatoes, halved
½ cup kalamata olives, drained
½ cup feta cheese, crumbled
Balsamic Vinaigrette Dressing:
¼ cup extra-virgin olive oil
1 Tbsp. balsamic vinegar
1 tsp. honey
¼ tsp. basil, dried
salt and pepper, to taste
Method

1. Whisk together oil, balsamic vinegar, honey, and basil in a small glass bowl. Set aside.
2. Place spaghetti, tomatoes, olives, and feta in a large salad bowl. Drizzle with dressing. Season with salt and pepper. Toss to combine well.
3. Transfer in individual plates.
4. Serve and enjoy.

Tuna Corn and Pasta Salad Recipe

This delicious pasta dish with tuna, corn, and sweet pepper is great for picnics and parties.

Preparation Time: 15 minutes
Total Time: 15 minutes
Yield: 2-3 servings
Ingredients
2 cups penne, cooked
8 oz. canned tuna flakes, drained
1 cup corn kernels

1 medium sweet red pepper, chopped

Lemon-Herb Vinaigrette Dressing:
¼ cup extra-virgin olive oil
2 Tbsp. lemon juice
¼ tsp. dried parsley
¼ tsp. dried basil
salt and pepper, to taste

Method
1. Whisk together oil, lemon juice, parsley, and basil in a small glass bowl. Set aside.
2. Place penne, tuna, corn, and pepper in a large salad bowl. Drizzle with dressing. Season with salt and pepper. Toss to combine well.
3. Transfer in individual plates.
4. Serve and enjoy.

Spicy Pasta Salad with Feta and Basil Recipe

This pasta recipe has been in the family for years, it makes a great lunch, snack, or dinner.

Preparation Time: 15 minutes
Total Time: 20 minutes
Yield: 4-5 servings

Ingredients
1 lb. penne, dry
2 cups fresh sweet basil leaves
2 medium celery stalks, chopped
1 shallot, chopped
1 cup feta cheese, crumbled
Spicy Balsamic Vinaigrette Dressing:
1/3 cup extra-virgin olive oil
2 Tbsp. balsamic vinegar
1 Tbsp. honey
2 tsp. chili flakes
1 tsp. cumin, ground
salt and pepper, to taste

Method
1. Bring large stock pot of salted water to a boil. Cook pasta for 10-12 minutes. Drain. Set aside.
2. Meanwhile, whisk together oil, balsamic vinegar, honey, chilli, and cumin in a small glass bowl. Set aside.
3. Place penne, basil, celery, and shallot in a large salad bowl. Season with salt and pepper. Toss to combine.
4. Transfer in individual plates. Top with crumbled feta. Drizzle with dressing.
5. Serve and enjoy.

Spiral Pasta and Mixed Vegetable Salad Recipe

This light and lovely pasta dish is can be made in a flash!
Preparation Time: 15 minutes
Total Time: 25 minutes
Yield: 4-5 servings

Ingredients
1 lb. spiral pasta, dry
2 cup broccoli florets, cooked
1 cup cherry tomatoes, halved
2 medium celery stalks, chopped
1 shallot, chopped
Balsamic Vinaigrette Dressing:
½ cup extra-virgin olive oil
2 Tbsp. balsamic vinegar
1 Tbsp. honey
½ tsp. basil, dried
salt and pepper, to taste
Method

1. Bring large stock pot of salted water to a boil. Cook pasta for 10-12 minutes. Drain. Set aside.
2. Meanwhile, whisk together oil, balsamic vinegar, honey, and basil in a small glass bowl. Set aside.
3. Place pasta, broccoli, cherry tomatoes, celery, and shallot in a large salad bowl. Season with salt and pepper. Toss to combine.
4. Transfer in individual plates. Drizzle with dressing.
5. Serve and enjoy.

Easy Chicken Macaroni Salad Recipe

This awesome macaroni salad with chicken makes a nice lunch or snack!
Preparation Time: 20 minutes
Total Time: 20 minutes
Yield: 6 servings
Ingredients
4 cups macaroni, cooked
12 oz. cooked chicken breast fillet, shredded
1 medium hard-boiled egg, chopped
2 medium celery stalks, chopped
1 shallot, chopped
½ cup mayonnaise
½ cup Greek yogurt
¼ cup cheddar cheese, grated
2 Tbsp. fresh chives
salt and pepper, to taste
Method
1. In a small bowl, mix together mayonnaise, yogurt, and chives.

2. Place macaroni, chicken, egg, celery, and shallot in a large bowl.
3. Add the dressing and cheese. Toss to coat. Season with salt and pepper. Transfer in a container with lid. Cover and chill until ready to serve.
4. Enjoy.

Cheesy Pasta Salad with Egg Recipe

This wonderful pasta dish with egg, cheese, and Greek yogurt makes a great breakfast or brunch item.

Preparation Time: 20 minutes
Total Time: 20 minutes
Yield: 5-6 servings
Ingredients
4 cups elbow macaroni, cooked
4 medium hard-boiled egg, chopped
2 medium celery stalks, chopped
1 medium carrot, chopped
1 shallot, chopped
1 cup Greek yogurt
2 Tbsp. lemon juice

1 tsp. lemon zest, grated
2 tsp. honey
½ cup cheddar cheese, grated
salt and pepper, to taste

Method
1. In a small bowl, mix together yogurt, lemon juice, lemon zest, and honey.
2. Place macaroni, egg, celery, carrot, and shallot in a large bowl.
3. Add yogurt dressing and cheese. Toss to coat. Season with salt and pepper. Transfer in a container with lid. Cover and refrigerate until ready to serve.
4. Enjoy.

Arugula and Pasta Salad with Pesto Sauce Recipe

Treat yourself and your loved ones with this scrumptious pasta salad with arugula and pesto!
Preparation Time: 20 minutes

Total Time: 20 minutes
Yield: 2-3 servings

Ingredients

2 cups penne, cooked
2 cups arugula (baby rocket)
1 medium tomato, thinly sliced
1 medium red bell pepper, cut into strips
¼ cup pesto sauce
2 Tbsp. pine nuts, toasted
2 Tbsp. parmesan cheese
salt and pepper, to taste

Method

1. Place penne, arugula, tomato, and pepper in a large bowl. Season with salt and pepper. Toss to combine. Divide in serving bowls. Sprinkle with parmesan and pine nuts. Drizzle with pesto sauce.
2. Serve immediately and enjoy.

Part 2

Meat Pasta Sauces

Awesome Sauce

"I only know how to make this marinara sauce in a three-gallon batch because after all my family members take their share it is all gone!"

Serving: 96 | Prep: 5 m | Cook: 30 m | Ready in: 35 m

Ingredients
- 3 gallons water
- 3 cups white sugar
- 1 (16 ounce) can tomato paste (such as Contadina®)
- 1 cup dried basil
- 1 cup dried minced onion
- 1/4 cup dried oregano
- 1/4 cup granulated garlic
- 1/4 cup salt
- 1 1/2 teaspoons cayenne pepper
- 1 pork neck

Direction
- Stir water, sugar, tomato paste, basil, minced onion, oregano, granulated garlic, salt, cayenne pepper, and pork neck together in a large pot.
- Bring the mixture to a simmer and cook until thickened to desired consistency, about 30 minutes.
- Remove pork neck bones to serve.

Nutrition Information
- Calories: 33 calories
- Total Fat: 0.1 g

- Cholesterol: < 1 mg
- Sodium: 41 mg
- Total Carbohydrate: 8.2 g
- Protein: 0.5 g

Bobbies Spaghetti Sauce

"This sauce is so amazing. I was trying to think of a good sauce without having too much of a tomato taste, and this does it. The mixture of veggies and seasonings does it. To make this more spicy, you can add fresh chiles or hot red peppers crushed. I don't like really hot food, so this was perfect for us. The vinegar makes it have a bit of a bite to it. You can add a bit more or less depending on your taste. Boil 2 pounds noodles; when done, pour sauce over noodles on your plate."

Serving: 8 | Prep: 20 m | Cook: 2 h 20 m | Ready in: 2 h 40 m

Ingredients
- 2 teaspoons olive oil
- 1 (12 ounce) package pork sausage links
- 1/2 pound ground beef
- 1 cup fresh mushroom slices
- 1 red bell pepper, chopped
- 1 yellow bell pepper, chopped
- 1/2 large onion, chopped
- 1 (16 ounce) can tomato sauce (such as Hunt's®)
- 1 (10 ounce) can diced tomatoes with green chile peppers
- 1 (8 ounce) can tomato paste
- 4 teaspoons balsamic vinegar
- 1 pinch dried oregano
- 1 pinch dried basil

- 1 pinch ground thyme
- 1 pinch kosher salt
- 1 pinch ground black pepper
- 1 pinch dried marjoram

Direction

- Heat olive oil in a large pot. Cook sausage links and ground beef in the hot oil until the sausages are cooked through and no longer pink in the center, 3 to 5 minutes per side. Stir mushrooms, red bell pepper, yellow bell pepper, and onion into the meat mixture; cook and stir until the vegetables are tender, 5 to 7 minutes.
- Remove sausages from pot to a cutting board to cool slightly; cut into bite-size pieces and return to the pot. Add tomato sauce, diced tomatoes with green chile peppers, tomato paste, balsamic vinegar, oregano, basil, thyme, kosher salt, black pepper, and marjoram to the pot; stir. Reduce heat to low and cook at a simmer, stirring every so often, for 2 to 3 hours.

Nutrition Information

- Calories: 199 calories
- Total Fat: 10.9 g
- Cholesterol: 46 mg
- Sodium: 886 mg
- Total Carbohydrate: 13.4 g
- Protein: 13.4 g

Bolognese Meat Sauce in Instant Pot

"Traditional Italian meat sauce (ragu) prepared in an Instant Pot®. When cooking in an Instant Pot®, the amount of liquid is minimal, so there is no additional water or broth required for this recipe. The final consistency is thick enough to toss with pasta, not too runny. Cooks much faster than traditional stovetop version! Just toss with pasta and serve."

Serving: 6 | Prep: 15 m | Cook: 1 h 32 m | Ready in: 1 h 52 m

Ingredients
- 2 tablespoons olive oil
- 1 onion, chopped
- 1 carrot, chopped
- 1 stalk celery, chopped
- 1 (16 ounce) package ground beef
- 1/2 pound ground pork
- 1/2 cup red wine
- 1 cup passata (crushed tomatoes)
- 2 tablespoons tomato paste
- salt and ground black pepper to taste
- 1/2 cup whole milk

Direction
- Turn on a multi-functional pressure cooker (such as Instant Pot(R)) and select Sauté function. Add olive oil, onion, carrot, and celery. Cook and stir until

vegetables start softening, about 5 minutes. Add ground beef and pork; cook until meat is no longer pink and juices evaporate, about 7 minutes. Pour in wine; cook until liquid evaporates, 10 to 15 minutes. Add passata, tomato paste, salt, and pepper.
- Close and lock the lid. Set Instant Pot(R) on Pressure Cook function; select high pressure according to manufacturer's instructions. Set timer for 1 hour. Allow 10 to 15 minutes for pressure to build.
- Release pressure carefully using the quick-release method according to manufacturer's instructions, about 5 minutes. Unlock and remove lid. Add milk; stir until absorbed into the sauce.

Nutrition Information
- Calories: 335 calories
- Total Fat: 22.5 g
- Cholesterol: 73 mg
- Sodium: 207 mg
- Total Carbohydrate: 8.3 g
- Protein: 21 g

Bolognese Sauce with Meat

"A recipe for your basic tomato and meat sauce. Serve with your favorite pasta and a nice loaf of sourdough bread."

Serving: 4

Ingredients
- 1/4 cup olive oil
- 1 onion, chopped
- 2 cloves garlic, minced
- 1 pound lean ground beef
- 1/4 pound thinly sliced prosciutto, chopped
- 4 tablespoons butter
- 2 roma (plum) tomatoes, chopped
- 1/4 cup tomato paste
- 1 teaspoon salt
- 1 teaspoon ground black pepper

Direction
- In a large saucepan sauté the onion and garlic in the olive oil. Add ground beef and continue cooking. Stir in prosciutto and cook for 5 to 6 minutes. Add 2 tablespoons of the butter, chopped tomatoes, and tomato paste. Let sauce simmer for 10 minutes. Season with salt and pepper.
- Simmer for one hour. Add additional butter and simmer for an additional half hour.

Nutrition Information
- Calories: 659 calories

- Total Fat: 57.6 g
- Cholesterol: 141 mg
- Sodium: 1423 mg
- Total Carbohydrate: 7.7 g
- Protein: 27.1 g

Brians Favorite Sauce

"A favorite spaghetti sauce with my sons - especially Brian. Serve over your favorite pasta. Simmering the sauce for longer will result in a deeper flavor. Adjust the seasonings as you like."

Serving: 6

Ingredients
- 1 onion, chopped
- 6 tablespoons olive oil
- 2 cloves garlic, minced
- 1 pound sweet Italian sausage, casings removed
- 2 (15 ounce) cans tomato sauce
- 1/2 teaspoon ground black pepper
- 1/2 teaspoon dried oregano
- 1 teaspoon dried basil
- 4 (16 ounce) cans diced tomatoes
- 1 teaspoon salt
- 2 tablespoons white sugar
- 1 pinch cayenne pepper

Direction
- In a large saucepan over medium heat sauté chopped onion and garlic in the oil. Break up sausage into small pieces and brown. Add tomato sauce, ground black pepper, dried oregano, dried basil, chopped tomatoes, salt, sugar and cayenne pepper; stir well. Let simmer uncovered 15 to 30 minutes.

Nutrition Information
- Calories: 501 calories
- Total Fat: 37.5 g
- Cholesterol: 58 mg
- Sodium: 2374 mg
- Total Carbohydrate: 24.2 g
- Protein: 15.4 g

Chef Johns Sunday Pasta Sauce

"This sauce goes by many names, including Sunday sauce, since that's the day it's traditionally made, but for me growing up, this was just called 'sauce.' As long as you cook the meat long enough, and season thoughtfully, there's really no way this sauce isn't going to be great. So, while you may not have grown up in an Italian-American home, with this comforting sauce simmering on the stove every Sunday, your family still can. Serve the sauce over pasta and top with the tender meat."

Serving: 10 | Prep: 30 m | Cook: 4 h 20 m | Ready in: 4 h 50 m

Ingredients
- 2 tablespoons olive oil, divided
- 1 (1 inch thick) slice beef shank
- 2 pounds pork spareribs
- 2 bone-in chicken thighs
- 1 onion, diced
- 1 pinch salt

- 6 cloves garlic
- 3 (28 ounce) cans crushed Italian (plum) tomatoes (such as San Marzano)
- 2 cups water, divided
- 1/4 cup tomato paste
- 1/4 cup freshly grated Parmigiano-Reggiano cheese
- 2 tablespoons chopped flat-leaf (Italian) parsley
- 2 teaspoons salt, or to taste
- 1 teaspoon ground black pepper
- 1/4 teaspoon red pepper flakes

Direction
- Preheat oven to 425 degrees F (220 degrees C).
- Drizzle 1 tablespoon olive oil in the bottom of a large roasting pan. Place beef, pork, and chicken in pan and turn to coat with olive oil.
- Roast in the preheated oven until meat is well browned, 20 to 30 minutes.
- Heat remaining 1 tablespoon olive oil in a large pot over medium heat. Cook and stir onion with a pinch of salt in hot oil until onion is soft and translucent, about 5 minutes. Add garlic; cook and stir until fragrant, about 1 minute.
- Pour crushed tomatoes, 1 1/2 cups water, and tomato paste into onion mixture. Add roasted beef, pork, and chicken to tomato sauce mixture.
- Pour remaining 1/2 cup water into the roasting pan, and bring to a boil while scraping the browned bits of food off of the bottom of the pan with a wooden spoon. Pour roasting pan water mixture into tomato mixture. Stir Parmigiano-Reggiano cheese, Italian

parsley, 2 teaspoons salt, ground black pepper, and red pepper flakes into tomato sauce; bring to a simmer, reduce heat to low, and simmer gently until sauce reduces and meat is tender, about 4 hours. Transfer meat to a dish. Adjust sauce seasonings to taste.

Nutrition Information
- Calories: 339 calories
- Total Fat: 19.6 g
- Cholesterol: 71 mg
- Sodium: 916 mg
- Total Carbohydrate: 20.3 g
- Protein: 23.2 g

Chunky Red Sauce with Ground Italian Sausage

"This is a basic chunky red sauce with Italian sausage and lots of veggies! Great for lasagna or your favorite pasta dish! Also, if you want the benefit of the veggies, but have picky eaters at your table, you can put it all in the food processor and they will never know the difference! I speak from experience!"

Serving: 10 | Prep: 15 m | Cook: 2 h 15 m | Ready in: 2 h 30 m

Ingredients
- 1 tablespoon extra-virgin olive oil
- 1 pound bulk Italian sausage
- 2 tablespoons minced garlic
- 1 onion, chopped
- 1 green bell pepper, chopped
- 1 sweet Italian pepper, chopped
- 1/2 teaspoon salt
- 1 zucchini, sliced
- 1 (28 ounce) can crushed tomatoes
- 2 (14 ounce) cans tomato sauce
- 1 (14.5 ounce) can diced tomatoes, drained
- 1 tablespoon tomato paste, or more as needed (optional)
- 2 teaspoons dried oregano
- 2 teaspoons dried basil
- 1 teaspoon onion powder
- 1 teaspoon chopped dried rosemary
- 1 teaspoon dried parsley

- 1/2 teaspoon ground black pepper
- 1/2 teaspoon red pepper flakes (optional)

Direction

- Heat olive oil in a large saucepan or Dutch oven over medium-high heat. Cook and stir sausage and garlic in hot oil until browned and crumbly, 5 to 7 minutes. Transfer sausage and garlic to a plate using a slotted spoon, leaving any drippings in the saucepan.
- Sauté onion, green pepper, sweet pepper, and salt in the same saucepan until slightly softened, about 5 minutes. Add zucchini and continue cooking until onion is translucent, 5 to 10 minutes more. Drain off any excess liquid.
- Stir sausage, crushed tomatoes, tomato sauce, diced tomatoes, tomato paste, oregano, basil, rosemary, parsley, black pepper, and red pepper flakes into onion-zucchini mixture. Bring to a simmer, reduce heat to low, cover the saucepan with a lid, and cook, stirring occasionally, until flavors blend and sauce is thickened, about 2 hours.

Nutrition Information

- Calories: 191 calories
- Total Fat: 10.4 g
- Cholesterol: 18 mg
- Sodium: 1093 mg
- Total Carbohydrate: 16.8 g
- Protein: 9.4 g

Classic Contadina Spaghetti Sauce

"This classic pasta sauce with lots of tomatoes and Italian sausage served on hot cooked pasta makes a quick, satisfying dinner any night of the week."

Serving: 6 | Prep: 10 m | Cook: 35 m | Ready in: 45 m

Ingredients
- 1 pound Italian sausage (casings removed), or extra lean ground beef
- 1 cup chopped onion
- 1 teaspoon minced garlic
- 1 (28 ounce) can CONTADINA® Crushed Tomatoes
- 1 (15 ounce) can CONTADINA® Tomato Sauce
- 1 cup chopped fresh mushrooms
- 1/2 teaspoon dried oregano
- 1/2 teaspoon dried basil
- 1/2 teaspoon salt
- 1/2 teaspoon sugar
- Cooked pasta

Direction
- Combine sausage, onion and garlic in a large skillet. Cook over medium-high heat 4 to 5 minutes or until sausage is no longer pink inside, stirring to break up sausage.
- Stir in crushed tomatoes, tomato sauce, mushrooms, oregano, basil, salt, sugar.

- Bring to a boil. Reduce heat to low; cook, uncovered, 30 minutes. Serve over hot cooked pasta.

Nutrition Information
- Calories: 605 calories
- Total Fat: 25.1 g
- Cholesterol: 58 mg
- Sodium: 1401 mg
- Total Carbohydrate: 69.8 g
- Protein: 23.9 g

Contadina Quick Bolognese Sauce

"For a quick weeknight dinner, this Bolognese sauce with ground beef and veggies, beef broth or wine is a perfect dish for families on the go."

Serving: 6 | Prep: 5 m | Cook: 20 m | Ready in: 25 m

Ingredients

- 1 pound lean ground beef
- 3 ounces bacon, chopped
- 1 cup chopped onion
- 1/2 cup sliced celery
- 1/2 cup chopped carrots
- 1/2 cup COLLEGE INN® Fat Free Lower Sodium Beef Broth, or red or white wine
- 1 (28 ounce) can CONTADINA® Crushed Tomatoes
- 3/4 cup whole milk

- Cooked pasta

Direction

- Brown beef, bacon, onion, celery and carrots in a large saucepan over medium-high heat until browned and crisp, about 10 minutes.
- Add broth; simmer until evaporated, scraping browned bits from bottom of pan.
- Stir in tomatoes and milk. Simmer over medium-low heat until sauce is thickened, about 15 minutes. Serve over pasta.

Nutrition Information

- Calories: 389 calories
- Total Fat: 13.2 g
- Cholesterol: 60 mg
- Sodium: 534 mg
- Total Carbohydrate: 40.4 g
- Protein: 25.5 g

Cubanelle and Veal Bolognese

"I have found myself making daily visits to Joseph's Classic Market these days and creating new recipes. Not only do we have amazing markets here in Palm Beach Gardens but our farmers markets are spectacular. I got 4 Cubanelle peppers and grilled 2 with our steak dinner. Looking at the remaining 2, this dish came to me. Enjoy with your favorite pasta, spaghetti squash, or sweet potato noodles."

Serving: 4 | Prep: 10 m | Cook: 50 m | Ready in: 1 h

Ingredients
- 2 tablespoons olive oil
- 2 Cubanelle peppers, chopped
- 2 cloves garlic, minced
- 1 pound ground veal
- 1/2 pound ground chuck
- 1 (28 ounce) can crushed tomatoes
- 1 tablespoon Italian seasoning
- 2 teaspoons sea salt
- 1 teaspoon ground black pepper

Direction
- Heat olive oil in a large saucepan over medium heat. Add Cubanelle peppers; cook and stir until softened, about 5 minutes. Stir in garlic; cook until fragrant, about 30 seconds.
- Stir veal and chuck into the saucepan; cook, breaking up gently with a wooden spoon, until browned, about 10 minutes. Add crushed tomatoes, Italian seasoning, salt, and pepper. Bring sauce to a boil; reduce heat to low and simmer, covered, until flavors combine, about 30 minutes.

Nutrition Information
- Calories: 351 calories
- Total Fat: 19.2 g
- Cholesterol: 106 mg
- Sodium: 1224 mg
- Total Carbohydrate: 17.1 g
- Protein: 29.6 g

Dads Spaghetti Sauce with Coffee

"Savory sauce with coffee. He would often smoke Italian sausage, and put it in in the last hour. Make plenty ahead of time, gets richer after a day or two."

Serving: 10 | Prep: 30 m | Cook: 1 h 15 m | Ready in: 1 h 45 m

Ingredients
- 3 tablespoons extra virgin olive oil
- 4 cloves garlic, slivered
- 2 large onions, sliced
- 1 large green bell pepper, sliced
- 2 tablespoons extra-virgin olive oil
- 1 1/2 pounds extra lean ground beef
- 2 (4 ounce) cans button mushrooms, drained
- 1 (16 ounce) jar spaghetti sauce with garlic
- 3 (8 ounce) cans tomato sauce
- 1 (6 ounce) can tomato paste, or to taste (optional)
- 1 tablespoon instant coffee granules
- 1 cup hot water

Direction
- Place 3 tablespoons of olive oil into a saucepan over medium heat, and cook the garlic in the oil for 1 minute. Stir in the onions, and cook until translucent, about 5 more minutes. Stir in the green bell pepper, and cook until the pepper begins to

- become tender, about 5 more minutes. Set the vegetables aside.
- Place 2 tablespoons of olive oil into a large saucepan over medium heat, and cook and stir the ground beef until the meat is no longer pink, about 10 minutes. Break the meat up into crumbles as it cooks. Mix in the mushrooms, spaghetti sauce, tomato sauce, tomato paste (if you prefer a thicker sauce), and vegetables. Bring the sauce to a boil, and reduce heat to a simmer. Cook, stirring occasionally, until the flavors have blended, about 30 minutes.
- Mix the coffee granules into the hot water, and pour into the sauce; simmer for 30 more minutes.

Nutrition Information
- Calories: 246 calories
- Total Fat: 11.7 g
- Cholesterol: 43 mg
- Sodium: 814 mg
- Total Carbohydrate: 18.2 g
- Protein: 18 g

Divine Spaghetti Sauce

"This is one of those all-day simmering beef, tomato and herb sauces. It is very good and very nutritious! Ingredients can be increased or lessened to your taste.

Freeze the remainder of sauce in plastic bags in serving sizes. Tastes better with each heating!!"

Serving: 7 | Prep: 30 m | Cook: 6 h | Ready in: 6 h 30 m

Ingredients
- 1 pound lean ground beef
- 2 (28 ounce) cans whole peeled tomatoes
- 2 (6 ounce) cans tomato paste
- 1 large onion, chopped
- 4 stalks celery, chopped
- 2 green bell peppers, chopped
- 1 red bell pepper, chopped
- 15 fresh mushrooms, sliced
- 5 tablespoons Italian seasoning
- 1 teaspoon dried red pepper flakes
- 4 bay leaves
- 2 tablespoons chopped fresh basil
- 3 cloves garlic, minced
- 1 pound spaghetti

Direction
- In a large skillet, brown beef over medium heat until no longer pink; cut up any remaining chunks of beef and reserve.
- In a large saucepan, combine whole tomatoes and paste; mash until smooth. Cover and heat on low.
- In a large skillet over medium heat, quickly sear onion and celery until transparent; add to tomato sauce in saucepan. In same skillet, sauté bell peppers and mushrooms for a few minutes, but do

not allow them to become soft; add to tomato sauce.
- Add Italian seasoning, dried red pepper flakes, bay leaves, basil and garlic to tomato sauce; add beef and mix. Remove cover, simmer over low heat and continue to simmer all day, stirring occasionally.
- Bring a large pot of lightly salted water to a boil. Add pasta and cook for 8 to 10 minutes or until al dente; drain.
- Add sauce to pasta; serve.

Nutrition Information
- Calories: 534 calories
- Total Fat: 15.6 g
- Cholesterol: 49 mg
- Sodium: 774 mg
- Total Carbohydrate: 75.7 g
- Protein: 26.3 g

Easy Carbonara Sauce

"Quick way to make a really tasty carbonara-style pasta sauce. Serve over cooked pasta."

Serving: 6 | Prep: 10 m | Cook: 20 m | Ready in: 30 m

Ingredients
- 6 ounces bacon, diced
- 1 large onion, diced
- 1 tablespoon minced garlic
- 1 (12 ounce) jar Alfredo sauce

- 1/2 cup water
- 3 roma (plum) tomatoes - halved, seeded, and chopped

Direction

- Cook bacon in a large skillet over medium-high heat until evenly browned, about 10 minutes. Drain all but about 2 tablespoons bacon drippings from skillet. Cook and stir onion with bacon in reserved drippings until onion is translucent, 5 to 10 minutes. Add garlic; cook and stir until fragrant, 2 minutes.
- Pour Alfredo sauce into onion-bacon mixture; rinse jar with the water and pour into skillet. Stir sauce with a wooden spoon, thoroughly scraping any brown bits of food from bottom of the skillet. Bring sauce to a simmer; add tomatoes. Simmer sauce until flavors blend, about 5 minutes.

Nutrition Information
- Calories: 231 calories
- Total Fat: 20.3 g
- Cholesterol: 33 mg
- Sodium: 761 mg
- Total Carbohydrate: 6.9 g
- Protein: 6.8 g

Eggplant Bolognese

"Italian recipes are my favorite especially when eggplant is included. This is a hearty bolognese and a paleo recipe that is prepared in one pot! You can add any of your favorite vegetables such as peppers or zucchini. You serve over spaghetti squash, zucchini noodles, or your favorite pasta! Enjoy!"

Serving: 6 | Prep: 15 m | Cook: 1 h | Ready in: 1 h 15 m

Ingredients
- 1/4 cup olive oil, divided
- 3 links pork sausage, casings removed
- 1/2 pound ground beef
- 2 pounds eggplant, peeled and chopped
- 1 small yellow onion, chopped
- 3 cloves garlic, minced
- 1 1/2 teaspoons sea salt
- 3/4 teaspoon freshly ground black pepper
- 1 (8 ounce) package sliced fresh mushrooms
- 1 (28 ounce) can crushed tomatoes
- 1 (12 ounce) can petite diced tomatoes
- 1 teaspoon dried parsley
- 1 teaspoon dried oregano
- 1 1/2 teaspoons dried basil

Direction
- Heat 2 tablespoons olive oil in a large Dutch oven over medium heat; cook pork sausage, breaking it onto smaller pieces with a wooden spoon, until browned, about 5 minutes. Add ground beef; cook and stir until beef is browned and crumbly, about 5 minutes. Drain excess fat.

- Pour remaining olive oil over sausage mixture; add eggplant, onion, garlic, salt, and black pepper. Cook and stir until lightly browned, about 10 minutes. Add mushrooms and continuing cooking until tender, about 5 minutes.
- Mix crushed tomatoes, diced tomatoes, parsley, oregano, and basil into sausage mixture; bring to a boil. Cover Dutch oven, reduce heat to medium-low, and simmer for 30 minutes.

Nutrition Information
- Calories: 282 calories
- Total Fat: 17.7 g
- Cholesterol: 34 mg
- Sodium: 840 mg
- Total Carbohydrate: 19.2 g
- Protein: 14.1 g

Enhance That Jar of Spaghetti Sauce

"I never have enough sauce from just a jar alone. I also like the taste of fresh ingredients. I like to combine both in this recipe! The red wine makes all the difference. Serve on favorite noodles with mozzarella cheese and mushrooms on top."

Serving: 20 | Prep: 20 m | Cook: 35 m | Ready in: 55 m

Ingredients
- 2 tablespoons butter
- 1 tablespoon extra-virgin olive oil
- 1 (8 ounce) package sliced fresh mushrooms
- 1 cup red wine, divided
- 1 pound ground beef
- 1 cup diced yellow onion
- 1 cup diced tomatoes
- 1/2 cup chopped red bell pepper
- 1/2 cup chopped green bell pepper
- 1/4 cup minced garlic
- 2 tablespoons oregano
- 2 tablespoons basil
- 1 tablespoon rosemary
- 1 (6 ounce) can tomato paste
- 1 (28 ounce) jar spaghetti sauce

Direction
- Melt butter with olive oil in a small skillet over medium-high heat. Cook and stir mushrooms in butter mixture until softened, 2 to 3 minutes. Add 1/4 cup red wine; bring to a simmer, reduce heat to

- medium-low, and cook until the mushrooms are very dark and shrunken in size, about 20 minutes.
- Heat a large pot over medium heat. Cook and stir ground beef, yellow onion, diced tomatoes, red bell pepper, green bell pepper, and garlic together until the beef is completely browned, about 10 minutes; season with oregano, basil, and rosemary. Stir 3/4 cup red wine and tomato paste into the beef mixture. Pour spaghetti sauce into the pot; stir. Return mixture to a simmer and continue cooking until the flavors blend, 10 to 30 minutes.

Nutrition Information
- Calories: 122 calories
- Total Fat: 5.7 g
- Cholesterol: 18 mg
- Sodium: 251 mg
- Total Carbohydrate: 10.2 g
- Protein: 5.7 g

Grandma Augustas Spaghetti Sauce

"This was passed down from my late Grandma Augusta to my mother and now me. It's an Americanized take on a nice Italian meat sauce for spaghetti, loaded with meat, tomatoes and other good things. Enjoy!"

Serving: 10 | Prep: 15 m | Cook: 45 m | Ready in: 1 h

Ingredients
- 3 slices bacon, diced
- 2 pounds lean ground beef

- 2 1/3 cups chopped onion
- 1/2 cup red wine
- 1 teaspoon salt
- 1 teaspoon dried basil
- 1 teaspoon dried oregano
- 1 teaspoon minced garlic
- 1/2 teaspoon ground black pepper
- 1 (12 ounce) can tomato paste
- 1 (28 ounce) can diced tomatoes
- 2 (16 ounce) cans tomato sauce
- 1/4 teaspoon hot pepper sauce (e.g. Tabasco™), or to taste

Direction

- Cook the bacon in a heavy, 5 quart pot over medium-high heat until the grease begins to render out, about 3 minutes. Stir in the ground beef and onions. Cook and stir until the beef is crumbly, and beginning to brown, about 10 minutes. Pour in the wine, and season with salt, basil, oregano, garlic, and pepper. Simmer uncovered until most of the wine has evaporated, about 10 minutes.
- Stir in the tomato paste, diced tomatoes, tomato sauce, and hot pepper sauce. Bring to a simmer, then reduce heat to medium-low, cover, and simmer 20 minutes.

Nutrition Information

- Calories: 280 calories
- Total Fat: 12.6 g
- Cholesterol: 63 mg
- Sodium: 1218 mg

- Total Carbohydrate: 18 g
- Protein: 22.1 g

Grandmas Homemade Italian Sauce and Meatballs

"This recipe has been handed down for generations and is always a hit. Both the sauce and meatballs freeze well. I freeze in dinner size portions so my husband and I don't have to use the bottled sauce!"

Serving: 10 | Prep: 1 h | Cook: 8 h | Ready in: 9 h

Ingredients
- 48 ounces tomato paste
- 12 cups water
- 2 cloves garlic, chopped
- 2 bay leaves
- 1 tablespoon dried basil leaves
- 1 teaspoon salt
- 5 pork chops
- 1 onion, diced
- 1 (8 ounce) package mushrooms, sliced
- 1 pound ground beef
- 1/4 pound ground pork
- 1/4 pound ground veal
- 1 cup grated Romano cheese
- 1 teaspoon salt
- 1/8 teaspoon black pepper

- 1 1/4 cups dry bread crumbs
- 2 cloves garlic, chopped
- 2 tablespoons dried parsley
- 2 eggs

Direction

- In a large pot combine tomato paste, water, garlic, bay leaves, basil, and salt. Bring to a boil, turn heat down to low and simmer.
- In a skillet, brown pork chops in olive oil then place in sauce mixture. Sauté onions and mushrooms in same pan that you browned the pork chops. Add these to sauce as well. Simmer sauce a minimum of 8 hours, stirring occasionally.
- To make the meatballs: Preheat oven to 350 degrees F (175 degrees C). Combine beef, pork, veal, Romano cheese, salt, pepper, bread crumbs, garlic, parsley and eggs; mix well. Shape into balls. Place on a baking sheet that has been sprayed with cooking spray.
- Bake meatballs for 20 minutes. Place meatballs in a serving bowl when baking is complete and place in refrigerator. About 2 hours prior to dinnertime pop the meatballs into the sauce.

Nutrition Information

- Calories: 422 calories
- Total Fat: 17.6 g
- Cholesterol: 111 mg
- Sodium: 1908 mg
- Total Carbohydrate: 38.5 g
- Protein: 31.4 g

Grandmas Meat Sauce

"This is a great meaty pasta sauce recipe passed down through the generations from my great great grandfather in Sicily. I also use this sauce when I make my lasagna. I don't like large chunks of meat in my sauce, so I put it all in the food processor when done and it comes out as a very thick meaty sauce."

Serving: 12 | Prep: 15 m | Cook: 2 h 45 m | Ready in: 3 h

Ingredients
- 1 tablespoon olive oil
- 1 pound sweet Italian sausage, sliced
- 1 pound round steak, cubed
- 1 pound veal, cubed
- 4 cloves garlic, chopped
- 2 (28 ounce) cans whole peeled tomatoes, crushed
- 1 tablespoon Italian seasoning
- 1 bay leaf
- 1/2 teaspoon garlic powder
- 1/2 teaspoon dried oregano
- 1/2 teaspoon ground black pepper
- 1/2 teaspoon dried parsley
- 1 (28 ounce) can tomato sauce

Direction
- Heat the olive oil in a skillet over medium heat, and cook the sausage, round steak, and veal 10 minutes,

until evenly browned. Remove meat from skillet and drain, reserving about 1 tablespoon drippings.
- Stir the garlic into the skillet with the reserved meat drippings, and cook about 3 minutes over medium heat. Place the crushed tomatoes into the skillet. Season with Italian seasoning, bay leaf, garlic powder, oregano, pepper, and parsley. Cook 15 minutes.
- Mix the tomato sauce into the skillet, and continue cooking 15 minutes.
- Return the meat to the skillet. Reduce heat to low, and simmer 2 hours, stirring occasionally.

Nutrition Information
- Calories: 217 calories
- Total Fat: 12.4 g
- Cholesterol: 53 mg
- Sodium: 871 mg
- Total Carbohydrate: 10.6 g
- Protein: 16.7 g

Grandmas Old Italian Spaghetti Sauce with Meatballs

"Grandma's sauce is an old recipe that she brought over from Italy. It is a long process with strange ingredients, but they all come together to make the best sauce I have ever had. The long process is worth your trouble the minute you take your first bite."

Serving: 12 | Prep: 1 h 30 m | Cook: 6 h 30 m | Ready in: 8 h

Ingredients
- 2 tablespoons olive oil
- 3 whole garlic cloves, peeled
- 2 pig's feet
- 1 pound pork neck bones
- 2 (6 ounce) cans tomato paste
- 1 1/2 cups water
- 2 (28 ounce) cans tomato puree
- 1 tablespoon white sugar
- 1 teaspoon black pepper
- 3/4 teaspoon baking soda
- 1 (16 ounce) loaf fresh Italian bread, torn into 2-inch pieces
- 1 cup water
- 6 eggs, beaten
- 1 pound ground pork
- 1 pound ground veal
- 1 pound ground beef
- 1 tablespoon olive oil
- 1 clove garlic, minced
- 2 tablespoons chopped fresh basil
- salt and pepper to taste
- 6 hard-boiled eggs, peeled (optional)

Direction
- Heat 2 tablespoons of olive oil over medium heat in the bottom of a large saucepan, and fry the garlic cloves 5 to 8 minutes, until brown and fragrant.

Remove the garlic cloves and set aside. Place the pig's feet and pork neck bones in the saucepan and fry, turning occasionally, until the meat and bones have browned, about 15 minutes.
- Return the garlic cloves to the saucepan, and stir in the tomato paste and 1 1/2 cups of water. Bring to a boil, and pour in the tomato puree. Reduce heat to low, and simmer for about 3 hours, stirring from the bottom often to prevent burning, until the pig's feet are tender and the mixture begins to thicken. Stir in the sugar, pepper, and baking soda. Continue to simmer while you prepare the meatballs.
- Soak the torn bread with 1 cup of water in a bowl. Squeeze excess water out of the bread, and place the bread in a large bowl with the 6 beaten eggs, ground pork, ground veal, and ground beef. Mix thoroughly and form into 24 meatballs about 2 1/2 inches in diameter.
- Heat 1 tablespoon olive oil in a large skillet over medium heat, stir in the minced garlic and chopped fresh basil, let them cook for about 1 minute, and then add the meatballs. Season with salt and pepper to taste, and fry them on all sides until brown, about 15 minutes, working in batches, if necessary.
- Place the browned meatballs, along with the oil, garlic, and basil from the skillet into the sauce, stirring lightly to avoid breaking them. Add the whole hard-boiled eggs, and simmer for about 1 1/2

more hours, until the meatballs are cooked, the sauce is thick, and all the flavors have blended.

Nutrition Information
- Calories: 599 calories
- Total Fat: 29.4 g
- Cholesterol: 319 mg
- Sodium: 1437 mg
- Total Carbohydrate: 38 g
- Protein: 46.2 g

Hearty Meat Sauce

"My grandmother fixed this for us growing up and I love it. It is a thick and hearty sauce for spaghetti or your favorite noodle! Of course the bread of choice would have to be Texas garlic bread!"

Serving: 4 | Prep: 15 m | Cook: 30 m | Ready in: 45 m

Ingredients
- 1/2 pound ground beef
- 2 (16 ounce) jars spaghetti sauce
- 1 diced yellow pepper
- 1 diced red bell pepper
- 1 (14.5 ounce) can peeled and diced tomatoes, drained
- 6 fresh mushrooms, coarsely chopped

Direction

- In a skillet over medium heat, brown the ground beef until no pink shows; drain.
- In a large pot combine browned beef and spaghetti sauce over medium heat for 5 or 10 minutes. Add yellow peppers, red peppers, canned tomatoes and mushrooms. Lower heat and simmer covered for 30 minutes, stirring every once in a while.

Nutrition Information
- Calories: 351 calories
- Total Fat: 14 g
- Cholesterol: 39 mg
- Sodium: 1111 mg
- Total Carbohydrate: 39.3 g
- Protein: 15.8 g

How to Make Bolognese Sauce

"This Bolognese sauce is dedicated to the late great Marcella Hazan. She was considered the Julia Child of Italian food, and at a time when most Americans thought 'Bolognese' was spaghetti sauce with chunks of hamburger, Marcella taught us just how magnificent this meat sauce could be. I like to toss it with some mezzi rigatoni and serve it with a little grated Parmesan cheese and a sprinkle of parsley."

Serving: 6 | Prep: 15 m | Cook: 3 h 20 m | Ready in: 3 h 35 m

Ingredients

- 2 tablespoons butter
- 1 tablespoon olive oil
- 1 cup finely diced onion
- 1/2 cup finely diced celery
- 1/2 cup finely diced carrot
- 1 pinch salt
- 1 1/2 pounds ground beef
- salt
- freshly ground black pepper to taste
- 1 pinch cayenne pepper, or to taste
- 1/8 teaspoon ground nutmeg
- 1 1/2 cups 2% milk
- 2 cups white wine
- 1 (28 ounce) can whole Italian plum tomatoes (preferably San Marzano)
- 2 cups water, or as needed

Direction

- Melt butter with olive oil in a large saucepan over medium heat; cook onion, celery, and carrot with pinch of salt until onion turns translucent, about 5 minutes. Stir ground beef into vegetables and cook, stirring constantly until meat is crumbly and no longer pink, about 5 minutes. Season meat mixture with 1 1/2 teaspoon salt, black pepper, cayenne pepper, and nutmeg.
- Pour milk into ground beef mixture and bring to a simmer. Cook, stirring often, until most of the milk has evaporated and bottom of pan is still slightly saucy, about 5 minutes.

- Raise heat to medium high and pour white wine into ground beef mixture; cook and stir until white wine has mostly evaporated, about 5 more minutes.
- Pour tomatoes with juice into a large mixing bowl and crush them with your fingers until they resemble a slightly chunky sauce. Pour tomatoes into sauce; fill can with 2 cups water and add to sauce. Bring to a simmer.
- Reduce heat to low and simmer, stirring often, until mixture cooks down into a thick sauce, at least 3 hours but preferably 4 to 6 hours. Skim fat from top of sauce if desired. If sauce is too thick or too hot on the bottom, add a little more water. Taste and adjust seasonings before serving.

Nutrition Information
- Calories: 394 calories
- Total Fat: 20.9 g
- Cholesterol: 84 mg
- Sodium: 935 mg
- Total Carbohydrate: 14.2 g
- Protein: 22.6 g

Italian Meat Sauce I

"Hearty sauce with sausage, pork and meatballs. It takes a while, but it's well worth it."

Serving: 12 | Prep: 45 m | Cook: 5 h | Ready in: 5 h 45 m

Ingredients

- 4 tablespoons olive oil
- 1 onion, chopped
- 6 cloves garlic, sliced
- 3 (15 ounce) cans seasoned tomato sauce
- 3 (14.5 ounce) cans diced tomatoes with juice
- 6 cups water
- 8 (6 ounce) cans tomato paste
- 2 pounds sweet Italian sausage
- 2 pounds ground sirloin
- 4 tablespoons chopped fresh parsley, divided
- 1 cup grated Romano cheese
- 2 tablespoons dried oregano
- salt and pepper to taste
- 1 pound pork meat, cubed
- 1 cup dry bread crumbs
- 3 tablespoons garlic powder
- 1/3 cup grated Parmesan cheese
- 2 eggs

Direction
- In large pot heat 2 tablespoons olive oil over low heat. Add chopped onion and two-thirds of sliced garlic. Sauté 5 minutes. Add tomato sauce, diced tomatoes, water and tomato paste. Simmer.
- Meanwhile, in large skillet, heat remaining 2 tablespoons of olive oil over medium heat. Sauté remaining garlic 1 to 2 minutes. Add sausage and brown, about three minutes on each side. After browning, cover and reduce heat. Cook for 10

minutes, remove from heat, and cut sausages into halves. Add to tomato mixture.
- Cook pork over medium heat in sausage skillet until brown. Add to tomato mixture. Add 3 tablespoons parsley, Romano, oregano, salt and pepper to tomato sauce. Continue to simmer over low heat.
- Preheat oven to 375 degrees F (190 degrees C). Cover a cookie sheet with aluminum foil. In large bowl combine ground sirloin, bread crumbs, garlic powder, remaining parsley, parmesan and eggs. Form 1 inch balls and place on cookie sheet. Cook until golden brown, about 20 minutes. Add meatballs to sauce. Continue to cook sauce for 5 hours. Serve over fusilli or ravioli.

Nutrition Information
- Calories: 661 calories
- Total Fat: 35.5 g
- Cholesterol: 134 mg
- Sodium: 2542 mg
- Total Carbohydrate: 46.4 g
- Protein: 41.9 g

Italian Meat Sauce II

"My standard sauce with meatballs, pork, and sausage. Delicious alone, on a sandwich, or over any pasta. Abruzzi recipe."

Serving: 10 | Prep: 45 m | Cook: 1 h 30 m | Ready in: 2 h 15 m

Ingredients
- 4 tablespoons extra virgin olive oil, divided
- 1 white onion, diced
- 3 cloves garlic, crushed
- 2 (28 ounce) cans crushed tomatoes
- 2 (28 ounce) cans whole peeled tomatoes
- 3/4 cup chopped Italian flat leaf parsley, divided
- 2 teaspoons garlic powder, divided
- 1 pound ground beef chuck
- 1 cup bread crumbs
- 1 egg
- 3 tablespoons milk
- salt and pepper to taste
- 1/2 pound hot Italian sausage
- 1/2 pound mild Italian sausage
- 1/2 pound pork neck bones
- 1/4 cup red wine (optional)

Direction
- Heat 2 tablespoons olive oil in a large saucepan over medium heat. Sauté onion and garlic until onion is soft and translucent. Pour in crushed tomatoes and whole tomatoes. As you are adding the whole tomatoes, let them slowly slide through your fingers and crush them coarsely on the way into the pot. Season with 1/4 cup of the parsley and 1 teaspoon garlic powder. Cover, and reduce heat to low.
- In a large bowl, mix the ground beef chuck, breadcrumbs, 1 teaspoon garlic powder, 1/8 cup parsley, egg, milk, and salt and pepper to taste. Mix ingredients with your hands until well blended.

Form into small, golf ball-size meatballs. Slice all of the sausage links but one hot and one mild link into 1/2 inch chunks.
- Heat 2 tablespoons in a large skillet over medium heat. The oil should be slightly smoking. Slice open the remaining links of hot and mild sausage, and crumble into the pan. Sauté, continually breaking up the pieces, until they are all golden brown. Transfer to the sauce. Brown the meatballs, chopped sausage links, and pork bones on all sides until they are a deep golden brown. You may need to do this in stages, and continually transfer into the sauce when browned. Drain excess fat.
- Pour the red wine into the skillet and deglaze all of the brown chunks on the bottom of the pan. Let the wine reduce to about half, then transfer into the sauce. Frequently stir, and season with salt and pepper to taste for about another hour after the last meat has been transferred into the pan. Finish by stirring the remaining fresh parsley into the sauce. Spoon sauce over your favorite pasta and serve the meat on a separate plate.

Nutrition Information
- Calories: 503 calories
- Total Fat: 31.8 g
- Cholesterol: 104 mg
- Sodium: 1037 mg
- Total Carbohydrate: 28.2 g
- Protein: 27.2 g

Italian Spaghetti Sauce with Meatballs

"This is a recipe I got from my mother years ago -- it's great."

Serving: 6 | Prep: 20 m | Cook: 2 h | Ready in: 2 h 20 m

Ingredients
- MEATBALLS
- 1 pound lean ground beef
- 1 cup fresh bread crumbs
- 1 tablespoon dried parsley
- 1 tablespoon grated Parmesan cheese
- 1/4 teaspoon ground black pepper
- 1/8 teaspoon garlic powder
- 1 egg, beaten
- SAUCE
- 3/4 cup chopped onion
- 5 cloves garlic, minced
- 1/4 cup olive oil
- 2 (28 ounce) cans whole peeled tomatoes
- 2 teaspoons salt
- 1 teaspoon white sugar
- 1 bay leaf
- 1 (6 ounce) can tomato paste
- 3/4 teaspoon dried basil
- 1/2 teaspoon ground black pepper

Direction
- In a large bowl, combine ground beef, bread crumbs, parsley, Parmesan, 1/4 teaspoon black

pepper, garlic powder and beaten egg. Mix well and form into 12 balls. Store, covered, in refrigerator until needed.
- In a large saucepan over medium heat, sauté onion and garlic in olive oil until onion is translucent. Stir in tomatoes, salt, sugar and bay leaf. Cover, reduce heat to low, and simmer 90 minutes. Stir in tomato paste, basil, 1/2 teaspoon pepper and meatballs and simmer 30 minutes more. Serve.

Nutrition Information
- Calories: 349 calories
- Total Fat: 21.2 g
- Cholesterol: 77 mg
- Sodium: 1492 mg
- Total Carbohydrate: 23.7 g
- Protein: 18.9 g

Italian Tomato Gravy

"This is my versatile Italian tomato gravy recipe. It goes great with spaghetti and meatballs as well on pizza."

Serving: 32 | Prep: 30 m | Cook: 11 h | Ready in: 11 h 30 m

Ingredients
- 1 cup red wine
- 1/4 cup olive oil
- 3 beef neck bones
- 1/2 yellow onion, chopped
- 1/2 cup chopped celery
- 1/2 carrot, chopped
- 1 whole head garlic, minced
- 2 tablespoons cracked black pepper
- 2 tablespoons red wine, or as needed
- 2 (6 ounce) cans tomato paste
- 4 (28 ounce) cans San Marzano-style peeled plum tomatoes with basil
- 2 (16 ounce) cans tomato sauce
- 1 quart water
- 1/2 cup dried basil
- 1/4 cup dried oregano
- 1 pinch dried Italian parsley

Direction
- Preheat oven to 400 degrees F (200 degrees C).

- Place 1 cup red wine, olive oil, beef neck bones, onion, celery, carrot, garlic, and black pepper in a roasting pan; stir to coat.
- Roast neck bones and vegetable mixture in the preheated oven until vegetables are tender, 1 hour. Stir in about 2 tablespoons red wine while scraping any browned bits of food off of the bottom of the pan. Roast until vegetables are browned, about 30 more minutes.
- Pour vegetable mixture into a 16-quart soup pot over medium-low heat; simmer for 30 minutes. Add tomato paste, plum tomatoes, tomato sauce, water, basil, oregano, and parsley; stir well. Simmer, stirring occasionally, until sauce reduces, 8 hours.
- Remove neck bones from sauce; scrape marrow out of bones. Add marrow to sauce and simmer until dissolved, 1 to 2 more hours.
- Transfer sauce to a blender in batches, filling blender no more than half full. Cover and hold lid down; pulse a few times before leaving on to blend. Puree until smooth.

Nutrition Information
- Calories: 63 calories
- Total Fat: 2 g
- Cholesterol: 0 mg
- Sodium: 377 mg
- Total Carbohydrate: 9.5 g
- Protein: 2 g

Italian Tomato Sauce

"The best spaghetti sauce! We had this every Wednesday when I was growing up. The secret ingredient is the nutmeg. Just a pinch. Delicious! Serve over spaghetti."

Serving: 10 | Prep: 20 m | Cook: 30 m | Ready in: 50 m

Ingredients
- 2 tablespoons olive oil
- 1 onion, diced
- 1/4 cup chopped celery (optional)
- 1 small garlic clove, minced
- 1 pound ground beef
- 40 ounces Italian-style stewed tomatoes
- 2 (6 ounce) cans tomato paste
- 1 (8 ounce) package sliced mushrooms, or to taste (optional)
- 1/2 cup grated Parmesan cheese, or to taste
- 1/4 cup parsley
- 1 1/2 teaspoons salt
- 1 teaspoon white sugar
- 1/4 teaspoon ground nutmeg
- 1/2 teaspoon dried oregano
- 1/8 teaspoon ground black pepper
- 1/4 teaspoon baking soda, or to taste

Direction
- Heat olive oil in a large pot over medium-high heat. Sauté onion, celery, and garlic in hot oil until softened, about 5 minutes; add beef and cook,

- stirring to break into small chunks, until no longer pink, 5 to 7 minutes more.
- Stir stewed tomatoes and tomato paste with the beef mixture until smooth; add mushrooms, Parmesan cheese, parsley, salt, sugar, nutmeg, oregano, and black pepper. Cook, stirring occasionally, until the sauce is flavorful, about 10 minutes.
- Stir baking soda into the sauce. Continue cooking until you can taste a reduction in acidity of the sauce, about 10 minutes more.

Nutrition Information
- Calories: 201 calories
- Total Fat: 9.6 g
- Cholesterol: 32 mg
- Sodium: 980 mg
- Total Carbohydrate: 17.6 g
- Protein: 12.6 g

Jansens Spaghetti Sauce and Meatballs

"I usually spend an afternoon preparing this and freeze leftovers in batches because it's that good. It will easily feed six or you can cut the entire recipe in half. Serve over your favorite spaghetti."

Serving: 6 | Prep: 45 m | Cook: 1 h 30 m | Ready in: 2 h 15 m

Ingredients
- Sauce
- 2 (28 ounce) cans chopped tomatoes
- 2 (6 ounce) cans tomato paste
- 2 (8 ounce) cans tomato sauce
- 4 teaspoons dried oregano
- 2 teaspoons dried parsley
- 1 teaspoon dried basil
- 2 teaspoons white sugar
- 1/2 teaspoon salt
- 6 cloves garlic, minced
- 2 tablespoons olive oil
- 1/4 cup red wine
- Meatballs
- 1 1/4 pounds ground meatloaf mix (beef, pork veal)
- 1 1/2 cups crushed corn flakes cereal
- 3 eggs
- 3 cloves garlic, minced
- 1/2 cup grated Parmesan cheese

- 3 tablespoons tomato paste
- 2 teaspoons dried oregano
- 2 tablespoons dried parsley
- 1 tablespoon white sugar
- 1/2 teaspoon garlic salt
- 1/2 teaspoon ground nutmeg
- 1/2 teaspoon ground black pepper

Direction

- For the sauce, combine the chopped tomatoes, 2 cans tomato paste, tomato sauce, 4 teaspoons oregano, 2 teaspoons parsley, basil, 2 teaspoons sugar, salt, 6 cloves garlic, olive oil, and red wine in a large, heavy pot. Cover, and cook over medium heat until bubbling. Uncover, reduce heat to low, and simmer for at least one hour, stirring often.
- Preheat an oven to 350 degrees F (175 degrees C). Coat a baking sheet with non-stick cooking spray.
- Combine the meatloaf mix, corn flakes, eggs, 3 garlic cloves, Parmesan cheese, 3 tablespoons tomato paste, 2 teaspoons dried oregano, 2 tablespoons dried parsley, 1 tablespoon sugar, garlic salt, nutmeg, and black pepper in a large bowl. Mix well with a large fork. Form the meat mixture into 1 1/2 inch firm balls. Place the meatballs on the prepared pan.
- Bake meatballs until browned and cooked through, about 20 to 30 minutes. Drop cooked meatballs into hot spaghetti sauce, and serve immediately.

Nutrition Information

- Calories: 416 calories

- Total Fat: 18.5 g
- Cholesterol: 148 mg
- Sodium: 1849 mg
- Total Carbohydrate: 40.2 g
- Protein: 26 g

Jeannes Slow Cooker Spaghetti Sauce

"This recipe has many vegetables and three kinds of meat. Most people can't tell it's not all beef and I've been told I ought to market it. This sauce has no acidic after taste, which is frequent with sauces that have tomato and/or bell pepper cooked over long periods of time. This sauce freezes well and can be used for other recipes."

Serving: 12 | Prep: 20 m | Cook: 3 h 20 m | Ready in: 3 h 40 m

Ingredients
- 1 (28 ounce) can crushed tomatoes
- 1 (28 ounce) can diced tomatoes
- 1 (6 ounce) can tomato paste
- 1 (10 ounce) can tomato sauce
- 1/2 pound turkey kielbasa, chopped
- 1/4 cup extra light olive oil
- 3 onions, chopped
- 6 yellow squash, diced
- 1 small green bell pepper, minced
- 3 cloves garlic, pressed
- 1/2 pound extra lean ground beef
- 1/2 pound extra-lean ground turkey breast
- 5 bay leaves
- 15 whole black peppercorns
- 1 1/2 teaspoons dried basil

- 1 teaspoon dried marjoram
- 2 teaspoons dried thyme
- 1/2 teaspoon dried oregano

Direction

- In a slow cooker, combine crushed tomatoes, diced tomatoes, tomato paste, tomato sauce, and kielbasa. Set slow cooker to High.
- Heat olive oil in a large, deep skillet over medium heat. Cook onions, squash, green pepper, and garlic in oil until onions are translucent. Transfer vegetables to the slow cooker.
- Place ground beef and ground turkey in a large, deep skillet. Cook over medium-high heat until evenly brown. Drain, crumble finely, and transfer to slow cooker. Season with bay leaves, peppercorns, basil, marjoram, thyme, and oregano.
- Cover, and cook on High for 2 hours. Remove lid, and cook 1 hour more.

Nutrition Information

- Calories: 212 calories
- Total Fat: 9.5 g
- Cholesterol: 38 mg
- Sodium: 624 mg
- Total Carbohydrate: 19.7 g
- Protein: 14.1 g

Kays Spaghetti and Lasagna Sauce

"This sauce came from a good friend's Italian mother-in-law. It is easy, and by far the best homemade sauce I know of. Great for both spaghetti and lasagna. Pssst...the secret is the sugar! Also, as I am now vegetarian, it tastes great with out the meat! Just substitute two tablespoons olive oil for the beef."

Serving: 8 | Prep: 20 m | Cook: 40 m | Ready in: 1 h

Ingredients
- 1 (28 ounce) can stewed tomatoes
- 1 (28 ounce) can crushed tomatoes
- 1 pound lean ground beef
- 2 yellow onions, chopped
- 2 green bell peppers, chopped
- 5 cloves garlic, chopped
- 2 tablespoons white sugar
- 1 tablespoon dried basil
- 1/2 teaspoon dried oregano
- salt and pepper to taste

Direction
- Blend the stewed tomatoes and crushed tomatoes in a blender. In a stock pot or large kettle, brown the ground beef with the onions, peppers, garlic. Pour in tomatoes, and reduce heat. Add sugar, basil and oregano, and simmer about 40 minutes. Season with salt and pepper before serving.

Nutrition Information

- Calories: 206 calories
- Total Fat: 8.4 g
- Cholesterol: 34 mg
- Sodium: 379 mg
- Total Carbohydrate: 22 g
- Protein: 13.2 g

Kicked Up Sausage Meat Sauce

"Italian sausage and ground beef, along with Ragu® Old World Style® Traditional Sauce and seasonings, make a delicious pasta sauce that's ready in under an hour."

Serving: 6 | Prep: 5 m | Cook: 40 m | Ready in: 45 m

Ingredients
- 1 pound Italian sausage, casings removed
- 1/2 pound ground beef
- 2 (24 ounce) jars RAGÚ® Old World Style® Traditional Sauce
- 1/2 cup chopped onion
- 3 cloves garlic, minced
- 1 tablespoon Italian seasoning
- Salt and pepper to taste
- Favorite pasta (optional)

Direction
- Heat a large, heavy pot over medium heat. Add the sausage, ground beef, and onion. Cook, stirring constantly, until the meat is completely browned.
- Stir in the Ragu(R) Old World Style(R) Traditional Sauce, garlic, and Italian seasoning. Bring to a simmer. Season with salt and pepper, if desired. Reduce heat to low and simmer for 20 to 25 minutes, stirring occasionally.
- Serve hot with your family's favorite pasta!

Nutrition Information
- Calories: 402 calories

- Total Fat: 23.5 g
- Cholesterol: 53 mg
- Sodium: 1523 mg
- Total Carbohydrate: 26.1 g
- Protein: 20.9 g

Lasagna Flatbread

"A simple lasagna pizza."

Serving: 6 | Prep: 25 m | Cook: 15 m | Ready in: 40 m

Ingredients

- 1 (15 ounce) container ricotta cheese
- 1 (8 ounce) package shredded mozzarella cheese, divided
- 1 (3 ounce) package Parmesan cheese
- 1 egg
- 2 teaspoons Italian seasoning
- 1 pound sausage
- 1/2 (26 ounce) jar marinara sauce
- 6 flatbreads

Direction

- Preheat oven to 375 degrees F (190 degrees C).
- Combine ricotta cheese, 1/2 of the mozzarella cheese, Parmesan cheese, egg, and Italian seasoning in a bowl.
- Cook sausage in a skillet over medium heat until no longer pink, 5 to 10 minutes; drain. Stir in marinara sauce.
- Spread 1/6 of the cheese mixture evenly on each flatbread; cover with sausage mixture. Top with remaining mozzarella cheese.
- Bake in the preheated oven until cheese is melted and bubbly, 10 to 15 minutes.

Nutrition Information
- Calories: 602 calories
- Total Fat: 36.8 g
- Cholesterol: 134 mg
- Sodium: 1679 mg
- Total Carbohydrate: 30.5 g
- Protein: 44 g

Lots OVeggies Sausage Spaghetti Sauce

"This Italian sausage and ground beef recipe is full of vegetables and Italian herbs -- the longer it cooks the better! Full of flavor, and makes a great base sauce for lasagna. It's critical to use fresh basil, other herbs may be dried. Do not use canned tomatoes which have any corn syrup in them. Home canned tomato equivalent is 3 quarts. If you want a spicier sauce add either crushed red pepper to taste or use hot Italian sausage."

Serving: 10 | Prep: 30 m | Cook: 3 h | Ready in: 3 h 30 m

Ingredients
- 1 pound sweet Italian sausage, casings removed
- 1 pound lean ground beef
- 1/4 cup olive oil
- 1 large onion, diced
- 1 green bell pepper, diced
- 1 red bell pepper, diced
- 1 zucchini, quartered and sliced
- 12 ounces mushrooms, sliced
- 2 carrots, shredded
- 4 ounces fresh basil, julienned
- 1 (10 ounce) package frozen chopped spinach, thawed and drained
- 1 tablespoon chopped fresh thyme
- 1 tablespoon fresh oregano

- 4 cloves garlic, crushed
- 1 tablespoon white sugar
- salt and pepper to taste
- 3 (28 ounce) cans peeled and diced tomatoes

Direction

- In a medium skillet over medium heat, cook sausage and ground beef until brown. Drain, reserving 2 tablespoons drippings. Set aside.
- In a large stock pot or Dutch oven heat oil over medium heat. Cook onions in oil until translucent. Stir in green and red bell peppers, zucchini, mushrooms and carrots and cook until just tender. Add browned sausage and ground beef. Stir in basil, spinach, thyme, oregano, garlic, sugar and salt and pepper. Cook 2 to 5 minutes. Pour in tomatoes, stir well, reduce heat, cover and simmer 3 hours, stirring occasionally.

Nutrition Information

- Calories: 339 calories
- Total Fat: 20.7 g
- Cholesterol: 45 mg
- Sodium: 803 mg
- Total Carbohydrate: 18.3 g
- Protein: 18.7 g

Ma Hunsickers Spaghetti Sauce

"Delicious, meaty, Italian pasta sauce. So good!"

Serving: 12 | Prep: 20 m | Cook: 2 h 10 m | Ready in: 2 h 30 m

Ingredients

- 2 pounds extra-lean (94%) ground beef
- 2 tablespoons butter
- 1/2 cup red wine
- 5 stalks celery, chopped
- 1 (8 ounce) package white mushrooms, sliced
- 1 onion, chopped
- 1 large green bell pepper, chopped
- 1 (28 ounce) can whole peeled tomatoes
- 1 (28 ounce) can tomato sauce
- 2 (6 ounce) cans tomato paste
- 6 cloves garlic, chopped
- 1 tablespoon white sugar
- 1 tablespoon dried oregano, or to taste
- 1 teaspoon seasoned salt (such as LAWRY'S®), or to taste
- 1 teaspoon Italian seasoning, or to taste
- 1 teaspoon dried parsley, or to taste

Direction

- Heat a large pot over medium-high heat. Cook and stir beef in the hot skillet until browned and crumbly, 5 to 7 minutes.
- Melt butter in a large skillet over medium heat. Cook and stir celery, mushrooms, onion, and bell pepper in hot butter until soft, 5 to 7 minutes; add to the ground beef.

- Stir whole tomatoes, tomato sauce, tomato paste, garlic, sugar, oregano, seasoned salt, Italian seasoning, and parsley into the beef and vegetable mixture; bring to a boil, reduce heat to low, and simmer, stirring frequently, until the sauce is thick and well-seasoned, 2 to 3 hours.

Nutrition Information
- Calories: 261 calories
- Total Fat: 12 g
- Cholesterol: 65 mg
- Sodium: 816 mg
- Total Carbohydrate: 17.2 g
- Protein: 21.1 g

Mama Palombas Spaghetti Sauce

"I got this recipe 30-plus years ago from a neighbor's mother who lived in Italy. It is delicious and always well received. Sub all or part of the ground beef and sausage for turkey or chicken products to lighten the recipe."

Serving: 16 | Prep: 30 m | Cook: 3 h 30 m | Ready in: 4 h

Ingredients

- 2 (28 ounce) cans plum tomato puree
- 1/2 pound hot Italian sausage, sliced into bite-sized pieces
- 1/2 pound mild Italian sausage, sliced into bite-sized pieces
- 2 pounds ground chuck
- salt to taste
- ground black pepper to taste
- 1 large onion, diced
- 3 cloves garlic, diced
- 1 1/2 cups water
- 1 (12 ounce) can tomato paste
- 1/4 cup grated Parmesan cheese
- 1 tablespoon dried basil, or to taste
- 1 tablespoon dried oregano, or to taste
- 1 tablespoon dried parsley, or to taste

Direction
- Heat tomato puree in a large pot over medium-low heat; simmer while prepared the remaining ingredients.
- Heat a skillet over medium heat; cook and stir hot Italian sausage, mild Italian sausage, and ground chuck until browned and cooked through, 10 to 15 minutes. Season with salt and pepper. Remove cooked sausage and chuck with a slotted spoon and transfer to the simmering tomato puree.
- Cook and stir onion and garlic in the same skillet used for browning meat until onions are lightly browned, 5 to 8 minutes. Transfer onion mixture to meat mixture.
- Stir water and tomato paste in the same skillet used for onion mixture over low heat until slightly thickened, about 15 minutes; add to the sauce in the pot. Sprinkle Parmesan cheese, basil, oregano, and parsley over the sauce; stir to combine. Simmer over low heat, stirring occasionally, for 3 hours.

Nutrition Information
- Calories: 215 calories
- Total Fat: 11.9 g
- Cholesterol: 37 mg
- Sodium: 828 mg
- Total Carbohydrate: 15.1 g
- Protein: 13.8 g

Maricas Spaghetti Meat Sauce

"Try topping your next bowl of pasta with this hearty spaghetti sauce. For added flavor, try stirring in diced smoked ham just before serving. Serve with your favorite pasta."

Serving: 4

Ingredients
- 2 tablespoons butter
- 2 onions, finely chopped
- 4 stalks celery, finely chopped
- 2 carrots, finely chopped
- 8 ounces lean ground beef
- 8 ounces ground pork
- 6 large ripe tomatoes, chopped
- 1 pinch dried oregano
- 1 pinch dried tarragon
- 1 pinch dried sage
- 1 pinch dried rosemary
- ground black pepper to taste
- salt to taste
- 2 bay leaves
- 8 ounces fresh mushrooms, sliced

Direction
- In a large skillet over medium heat sauté the finely chopped onions, carrot, and celery with the 2 tablespoons of butter or margarine. Add the beef and pork and cook until brown. Add chopped tomatoes, dried oregano, tarragon, sage, rosemary,

and bay leaves. Add salt and pepper to taste. Simmer for an hour.
- Near completion of cooking time add in mushrooms and simmer until softened, about 10 minutes.

Nutrition Information
- Calories: 552 calories
- Total Fat: 29.5 g
- Cholesterol: 86 mg
- Sodium: 1391 mg
- Total Carbohydrate: 47.4 g
- Protein: 28.4 g

Meat Gravy

"This recipe is a family tradition. It has been handed down from generation to generation but never written down. There are things I'd like to explain before starting: some of the meats I use are interchangeable. The whole idea of a meat gravy is the different combination of meats, not the exact meats themselves. The two basic meats are pork and beef; some like to add veal, but I don't. Many in my family add their own third meat: some use poultry, mine is lamb. Some in our family only use beef and pork but I find it less tasty. Serve the sauce over your favorite pasta with grated cheese; I recommend Locatelli® Pecorino Romano. I also add meatballs and braciole to the sauce; see links below for those recipes."

Serving: 30 | Prep: 1 h 30 m | Cook: 5 h | Ready in: 6 h 30 m

Ingredients
- 1/4 cup extra virgin olive oil
- 1 (2 1/2 pound) pork shoulder roast
- 24 cloves garlic, peeled and lightly cracked into large pieces (divided)
- 2 pounds pork spareribs
- 2 pounds beef oxtails, cut into pieces
- 1 lamb shank (optional)
- 8 (28 ounce) cans Italian-style whole peeled tomatoes
- 1 pound hot Italian sausage, casings removed
- 1 pound sweet Italian sausage, casings removed
- 3 (6 ounce) cans tomato paste
- 2 teaspoons salt, or to taste
- fresh ground black pepper to taste
- 1 pinch crushed red pepper flakes
- 1/2 cup Burgundy wine or other dry red wine
- 8 leaves basil, chopped

Direction
- Heat the olive oil in a large pot over medium-low heat. Place the pork shoulder in the center of the pot and arrange 4 or 5 garlic cloves around the sides of the pan.
- Brown the pork roast on all sides and transfer to a large baking dish; remove garlic cloves from pot with a slotted spoon and transfer to a bowl. Repeat the process, browning pork spareribs, oxtails, and

lamb shank, adding about 4 cloves of cracked garlic with each batch of meat, and transferring meats to the baking dish. Transfer each batch of garlic cloves to the bowl when cooked.

- While the meats are cooking, strain the cans of tomatoes and their juice. Use a food mill or press the tomatoes through a colander to remove all of the seeds and extra pulp. Discard seeds and pulp and transfer strained tomatoes to a large bowl; set aside.
- Cook the sausage in the olive oil in the same pot over medium heat until browned, breaking it up with a wooden spoon as it cooks, until no longer pink, 10 to 12 minutes. Transfer the cooked sausage to a large bowl and refrigerate while you complete the next steps. When all of the sausage is browned, return the reserved garlic cloves to the pot and stir in tomato paste, salt, black pepper, and red pepper flakes.
- Stir the tomato paste with a wooden spoon, scraping up the browned bits of meat in the pot. There will be a buildup of juices in the baking dish where the meats are resting; pour this liquid into the pot. Add the Burgundy wine and cook, stirring occasionally, until most of the liquid has evaporated, about 15 minutes.
- Pour in the strained tomatoes and juice and stir in the basil. Cover the pan and bring the sauce to a boil, stirring occasionally. Remove the lid and add the cooked pork shoulder, pork ribs, oxtails, and

lamb shank. Reduce the heat to low and simmer, stirring occasionally, for 4 to 5 hours. (If you're adding braciole, see Cook's Note.)
- Remove the pork shoulder, pork spareribs, oxtails, and lamb shank. When cool enough to handle, remove the meat from the bones and finely chop it. Return meats to the pot of sauce and discard the bones.
- Stir the cooked sausage into the sauce; simmer for an additional 1 hour. Taste the sauce and adjust the seasonings.

Nutrition Information
- Calories: 277 calories
- Total Fat: 16.7 g
- Cholesterol: 62 mg
- Sodium: 944 mg
- Total Carbohydrate: 11.7 g
- Protein: 19.1 g

Meatball Spaghetti Sauce

"Tasty seasoned meatballs simmered in a flavorful red sauce. For a creamier sauce, substitute milk for the water."

Serving: 6 | Prep: 30 m | Cook: 1 h | Ready in: 1 h 30 m

Ingredients
- 1 pound lean ground beef
- 1 cup dry bread crumbs
- 2/3 cup milk

- 1 egg
- 2 cloves garlic, minced
- 2 onions, finely chopped
- 1 teaspoon salt
- 1 teaspoon dried parsley
- 1/8 teaspoon black pepper
- 2 tablespoons olive oil
- 2 (10.75 ounce) cans condensed tomato soup
- 2 (10.75 ounce) cans water
- 2 tablespoons lemon juice
- 1/2 teaspoon salt
- 1 teaspoon dried parsley
- 1/2 teaspoon dried basil leaves
- 1/2 teaspoon dried sage
- 1/2 teaspoon dried thyme
- 1/4 teaspoon cayenne pepper

Direction

- To make meatballs: Combine in a bowl ground beef, bread crumbs, milk, egg, garlic, onions, salt, parsley and pepper; mix well. Roll into 1 inch balls and set aside.
- Heat oil in large skillet over medium heat; add meatballs and cook gently so they stay whole and are lightly browned.
- To make the sauce: Mix together tomato soup, water, lemon juice, salt, parsley, basil, sage, thyme and cayenne pepper in a large saucepan, add meatballs and simmer for 1 hour.

Nutrition Information

- Calories: 375 calories
- Total Fat: 18.9 g
- Cholesterol: 79 mg
- Sodium: 1433 mg
- Total Carbohydrate: 32.3 g
- Protein: 19.9 g

MeatLovers Slow Cooker Spaghetti Sauce

"This creates a great, chunky, and very meaty spaghetti sauce. The longer it cooks, the better it tastes!"

Serving: 8 | Prep: 20 m | Cook: 8 h 20 m | Ready in: 8 h 40 m

Ingredients
- 2 tablespoons olive oil
- 2 small onions, chopped
- 1/4 pound bulk Italian sausage
- 1 pound ground beef
- 1 teaspoon dried Italian herb seasoning
- 1 teaspoon garlic powder
- 1/2 teaspoon dried marjoram
- 1 (29 ounce) can tomato sauce
- 1 (6 ounce) can tomato paste
- 1 (14.5 ounce) can Italian-style diced tomatoes
- 1 (14.5 ounce) can Italian-style stewed tomatoes
- 1/4 teaspoon dried thyme leaves
- 1/4 teaspoon dried basil

- 1/2 teaspoon dried oregano
- 2 teaspoons garlic powder
- 1 tablespoon white sugar

Direction

- Heat olive oil in a skillet over medium heat; cook and stir onions and Italian sausage until the sausage is browned, about 10 minutes. Transfer the sausage and onions to a slow cooker. In the same skillet, cook and stir the ground beef, Italian seasoning, 1 teaspoon of garlic powder, and marjoram, breaking the meat up as it cooks, until the meat is browned, about 10 minutes. Transfer the ground beef into the slow cooker.
- Stir in the tomato sauce, tomato paste, diced tomatoes, stewed tomatoes, thyme, basil, oregano, and 2 teaspoons of garlic powder. Set the cooker on Low, and cook the sauce for 8 hours. About 15 minutes before serving, stir in the sugar. Serve hot.

Nutrition Information

- Calories: 264 calories
- Total Fat: 14.8 g
- Cholesterol: 45 mg
- Sodium: 1025 mg
- Total Carbohydrate: 18.8 g
- Protein: 15 g

Meaty Spaghetti Sauce

"Tired of the same old boring spaghetti sauce recipes? I invented this one to satisfy my craving for a meaty, flavorful sauce. Serve with your favorite pasta, topped with grated Parmesan cheese. Freeze the leftovers for a quick dinner another night!"

Serving: 32

Ingredients
- 1 pound lean ground beef
- 1 pound pork sausage
- 2 ounces sliced pepperoni sausage
- 1 green bell pepper, chopped
- 1/2 red bell pepper, chopped
- 1 tablespoon minced garlic
- 2 onions, chopped
- 2 carrots, diced
- 2 stalks celery, chopped
- 1 (8 ounce) can sliced mushrooms
- 1 (15 ounce) can tomato sauce
- 2 (14.5 ounce) cans diced tomatoes
- 2 (6 ounce) cans tomato paste
- 3 cubes beef bouillon cube
- 3 bay leaves
- 1 tablespoon dried thyme
- 1 1/2 tablespoons dried oregano
- 1 1/2 teaspoons dried basil

- 1/2 teaspoon crushed red pepper flakes
- 1 teaspoon ground black pepper
- 1 tablespoon white sugar
- 1 cup beef broth

Direction
- In a large stockpot cook the ground beef, sausage, pepperoni, green bell pepper, red bell pepper, garlic, onion, carrots and celery. Cook until beef is no longer pink. Drain into a large colander to drain grease.
- To the large saucepot, add the mushrooms, tomato sauce, tomatoes, tomato paste, bouillon cubes, bay leaves, thyme, oregano, basil, crushed red pepper, black pepper, sugar, and beef broth and stir well. Pour the meat mixture into the pot. Bring to a boil, reduce heat and cover. Simmer for 2 hours.

Nutrition Information
- Calories: 102 calories
- Total Fat: 6 g
- Cholesterol: 19 mg
- Sodium: 515 mg
- Total Carbohydrate: 6.3 g
- Protein: 6.2 g

Moms Quick Pasta Sauce

"This is my mom's incredible (well, to everyone that's tried it) spaghetti sauce that I use for most of my Italian-style dishes. Add herbs and extra water as you prefer or to suit the occasion. Serve over your favorite pasta, or use as a lasagna sauce."

Serving: 6

Ingredients
- 1 pound lean ground beef
- 1 1/3 (6 ounce) cans tomato paste
- 1 (15 ounce) can tomato sauce
- 1 (1 ounce) package dry onion soup mix
- 1 cup water
- 1/4 tablespoon dried basil
- 1/8 teaspoon garlic, minced
- 2 teaspoons dried oregano
- salt to taste
- ground black pepper to taste

Direction
- In a large skillet cook ground beef. Mix in the tomato paste, tomato sauce, onion soup mix, water, basil, garlic, oregano, salt, and ground black pepper.
- Simmer until heated through.

Nutrition Information
- Calories: 262 calories
- Total Fat: 16.1 g
- Cholesterol: 57 mg
- Sodium: 1130 mg
- Total Carbohydrate: 14.3 g
- Protein: 16.3 g

Moms Spaghetti Sauce

"This is a simple homemade tomato sauce and there is usually enough left for seconds. Just pop the leftover in the freezer. This sauce is also great for lasagna or terrific over your favorite pasta."

Serving: 8

Ingredients
- 1 pound lean ground beef
- 1 onion, chopped
- 4 tablespoons chopped fresh parsley
- 7 tablespoons olive oil
- 1 (46 fluid ounce) can tomato juice
- 1 1/2 (15 ounce) cans tomato sauce
- 2 teaspoons Worcestershire sauce
- 2 teaspoons salt
- 1 pinch ground black pepper
- 1/4 teaspoon garlic salt

Direction
- In a large skillet cook ground beef with the chopped onions, parsley, and olive oil. Cook until onions are soft and ground beef is cooked through.
- In a large saucepan, combine tomato juice, tomato sauce, Worcestershire sauce, salt, ground black pepper, and garlic. Add ground beef mixture and simmer for 1 hour.

Nutrition Information
- Calories: 308 calories
- Total Fat: 23.8 g

- Cholesterol: 43 mg
- Sodium: 1539 mg
- Total Carbohydrate: 12.8 g
- Protein: 12.5 g

Moms Sweet Spaghetti Sauce

"My mom has made this sauce ever since before I was born. My whole family and all my friends love it. I love it cause it's sweet and different from all the other spicy and tart sauces."

Serving: 7 | Prep: 30 m | Cook: 30 m | Ready in: 1 h

Ingredients
- 2 tablespoons vegetable oil
- 1/2 onion, minced
- 1/2 green bell pepper, chopped
- 1 pound ground beef
- 4 slices bacon
- 2 (4 ounce) jars mushrooms, drained
- 1 (29 ounce) can tomato sauce
- 1 (6 ounce) can tomato paste
- 2 tablespoons garlic powder
- 2 tablespoons dried oregano
- 1/2 cup white wine
- 3/4 cup sugar
- salt and pepper to taste

Direction

- In a skillet over medium heat, cook onion and bell pepper in oil until transparent. Add beef to onions and peppers; cook until brown. Set aside.
- Place bacon in a large, deep skillet. Cook over medium-high heat until evenly brown. Reserve drippings and crumble bacon. Combine drippings and crumbled bacon with the beef mixture.
- Add mushrooms, tomato sauce, tomato paste, garlic powder and oregano. Pour in wine while stirring. Stir in sugar, then salt and pepper. Cook until hot.

Nutrition Information
- Calories: 480 calories
- Total Fat: 28.9 g
- Cholesterol: 66 mg
- Sodium: 1117 mg
- Total Carbohydrate: 38.4 g
- Protein: 16.6 g

Nanas Slow Cooked Meaty Tomato Sauce

"Although my grandma was Danish, she was famous for her slow-cooked Italian tomato sauce. It cooks a long time, but is well worth the wait."

Serving: 12 | Prep: 30 m | Cook: 6 h 15 m | Ready in: 6 h 45 m

Ingredients
- 1 pound sweet Italian sausage, casings removed
- 1 pound hot Italian sausage, casings removed

- 1/2 pound ground beef
- 1 large onion, finely diced
- 1/4 cup minced garlic, or to taste
- 4 (14.5 ounce) cans diced tomatoes
- 2 (6 ounce) cans tomato paste
- 2 (14 ounce) cans tomato sauce
- 1/2 cup chicken broth
- 1/2 cup Cabernet Sauvignon (or other dry red wine)
- 1 tablespoon dried Italian herb seasoning
- 1/2 cup chopped fresh basil
- 1 teaspoon salt
- 1/2 teaspoon ground black pepper, or to taste

Direction

- Heat a large skillet over medium-high heat and stir in Italian sausage, ground beef, onion, and garlic. Cook and stir until the meat is crumbly, evenly browned, and no longer pink, about 15 minutes. Use a potato masher to mash and blend the meat mixture every few minutes. Drain and discard any excess grease.
- Stir in diced tomatoes, tomato paste, tomato sauce, chicken broth, red wine, Italian seasoning, basil, salt, and black pepper.
- Transfer the sauce to a slow cooker and cook on low for 6 to 8 hours.

Nutrition Information

- Calories: 289 calories
- Total Fat: 16.6 g
- Cholesterol: 47 mg

- Sodium: 1565 mg
- Total Carbohydrate: 18.6 g
- Protein: 17 g

North End Sunday Gravy

"This recipe takes some time but makes a delicious gravy that would make your Italian grandmother proud. The dried mint is not 'minty' at all but rather lends a sweetly herbal flavor to the sauce. You can leave out the lamb shank, but it is the secret ingredient that makes the sauce extra delicious. Many people prefer San Marzano® tomatoes, but they are expensive and I think our own domestic tomatoes actually make a better sauce."

Serving: 12 | Prep: 30 m | Cook: 5 h 30 m | Ready in: 6 h

Ingredients
- 1/4 cup olive oil
- 2 pork neck bones
- 1 country-style pork rib
- 1 (8 ounce) beef chuck in 1 piece
- 1 beef rib, or more to taste
- 1 lamb shank (optional)
- 1/4 cup olive oil
- 1 pinch dried basil, or to taste
- 1 pinch dried mint, or to taste
- 1 pinch red pepper flakes, or to taste

- 1 onion, chopped
- 1 clove garlic, minced
- 1 (12 ounce) can tomato paste
- 2 (28 ounce) cans crushed tomatoes
- 7 cups water, or as needed
- 2 pinches dried basil
- 2 pinches dried mint
- 2 pinches crushed red pepper flakes
- salt and ground black pepper to taste
- 2 tablespoons olive oil
- 1 pound bulk Italian sausage
- 1/2 tablespoon white sugar, or to taste
- 1 pound ground beef
- 1/4 pound ground pork
- 2 eggs
- 1/2 cup milk
- 1 cup Italian bread crumbs
- 1/2 cup chopped Italian flat leaf parsley
- 1/4 cup grated Parmesan cheese
- 1 clove garlic, minced
- 1 1/2 teaspoons olive oil

Direction

- Heat 1/4 cup olive oil in a stockpot over medium heat. Cook neck bones, country-style pork rib, beef chuck, beef rib, and lamb shank in hot oil, turning regularly, until browned on all sides, 7 to 10 minutes. Remove all the meat to a large bowl.
- Pour another 1/4 cup olive oil into the stockpot and heat over medium heat; stir a pinch of basil, a pinch

of mint, and a pinch of red pepper flakes into the oil. Cook and stir onions in hot oil until translucent, about 5 minutes. Add garlic; cook and stir 1 minute more. Stir the tomato paste into the onion mixture until incorporated. Pour crushed tomatoes and water into the mixture and bring to a low boil. Add an additional 2 pinches each of basil, mint, and red pepper flakes. Season with salt and black pepper.

- Return the browned meats to the tomato mixture; bring to a simmer and cook, stirring every 15 minutes, for 2 1/2 hours. Remove the neck bones and discard.
- Heat 2 tablespoons olive oil in a skillet over medium heat. Crumble Italian sausage into the skillet; cook and stir until crumbly, evenly browned, and no longer pink, 5 to 7 minutes. Drain and discard any excess grease. Stir sausage into the tomato sauce with sugar. Return the sauce to a simmer and cook another 1 1/2 hours.
- Mix ground beef, ground pork, eggs, milk, Italian bread crumbs, parsley, Parmesan cheese, and garlic with your hands in a large bowl until evenly mixed; shape into 2-inch balls.
- Heat 1 1/2 teaspoons in a skillet over medium heat. Cook the meat balls in hot oil until evenly browned, 5 to 7 minutes.
- Add meatballs to the tomato sauce. Cook at a simmer for 1 hour, adding water as needed to keep sauce from becoming too thick. Remove stockpot

from heat; let sit 2 to 3 minutes. Skim and discard any fat from the top of the sauce.

Nutrition Information
- Calories: 527 calories
- Total Fat: 35.8 g
- Cholesterol: 110 mg
- Sodium: 869 mg
- Total Carbohydrate: 25 g
- Protein: 28.4 g

North Italian Meat Sauce Ragu Bolognese

"This recipe comes from Bologna, Italy. One unusual characteristic of this sauce is that there is no garlic in it--but there is a hint of ground nutmeg. Serve over hot cooked pasta."

Serving: 28 | Prep: 25 m | Cook: 1 h 5 m | Ready in: 1 h 30 m

Ingredients
- 4 tablespoons butter, divided
- 4 ounces pancetta, diced
- 1 cup diced onion
- 1 cup chopped carrot
- 1/2 cup chopped celery
- 2 tablespoons olive oil

- 1/4 pound lean ground beef
- 12 ounces lean ground pork
- 1/2 cup white wine
- 2 cups beef stock
- 2 tablespoons tomato paste
- 1/2 pound chicken liver
- 1 cup heavy whipping cream
- 1 pinch ground nutmeg
- 1 teaspoon salt, or to taste
- 1/2 teaspoon freshly ground black pepper, or to taste

Direction

- In a large skillet, melt 2 tablespoons butter over medium heat. Add pancetta, onion, carrot, and celery and cook, stirring often, for 10 minutes or until lightly browned. Transfer to a heavy large saucepan.
- In same skillet, heat olive oil. Cook ground beef and pork over medium heat, stirring to break up any lumps, until browned. Pour in the wine, increase the heat and boil briskly, stirring constantly, until almost all of the liquid has evaporated. Transfer ground meat mixture to the saucepan with the pancetta and vegetables. Set skillet aside.
- Stir the beef stock and tomato paste into the saucepan. Bring sauce to a boil over high heat, then reduce the heat and simmer, partially covered, for 45 minutes, stirring occasionally.
- Meanwhile, melt remaining 2 tablespoons of butter over medium-high heat in the original skillet. Add

chicken livers and sauté for 3 to 4 minutes, or until firm and lightly browned. Remove livers from skillet and dice. Set aside and add to sauce 10 minutes before it is done. A few minutes before serving, stir in the cream and let it heat through. Season sauce with nutmeg, salt, and pepper to taste.

Nutrition Information
- Calories: 135 calories
- Total Fat: 11.5 g
- Cholesterol: 58 mg
- Sodium: 167 mg
- Total Carbohydrate: 1.9 g
- Protein: 5.3 g

Not Red Spaghetti Sauce

"A lovely Italian sausage and vegetable topping to serve over your spaghetti for a change of pace. Add pimento for a dash of color."

Serving: 6 | Prep: 20 m | Cook: 10 m | Ready in: 30 m

Ingredients
- 1 1/2 pounds Italian sausage
- 4 ounces fresh mushrooms, sliced
- 1/2 cup butter
- 2 cubes chicken bouillon
- 1/2 cup sherry
- 1 1/2 pounds zucchini, sliced
- 1/2 cup chopped green onion

- 1 (16 ounce) package spaghetti

Direction

- In large skillet, over medium heat, cook sausage and mushrooms in butter, until sausage is brown. Add bouillon cubes and sherry and stir until bouillon is dissolved. Add zucchini and onion and cook, uncovered, until zucchini is crisp-tender.
- While the sauce is cooking, bring a large pot of lightly salted water to a boil. Cook spaghetti in the boiling water, stirring occasionally until cooked through but firm to the bite, about 12 minutes. Drain.
- Serve pasta sauce over hot spaghetti.

Nutrition Information

- Calories: 726 calories
- Total Fat: 38.1 g
- Cholesterol: 85 mg
- Sodium: 1566 mg
- Total Carbohydrate: 67.3 g
- Protein: 26.9 g

Old Fashioned Sicilian Succo

"My Nana used to cook this for me when I was young and as she prepared things and we waited for the sauce to finish, she'd tell me great stories about her life in Sicily and other secret business! This recipe is the best sauce I've ever had- I really think it can bring the family together. Just prepare it and you'll see that when dinner time comes everyone's mouths will be watering because of the great smell, the entire family can gather around the table and there will be enough for everyone, I promise! Good for vegetarians too-just substitute 2 1/2 pounds of chopped zucchini for the meatballs."

Serving: 20 | Prep: 30 m | Cook: 4 h | Ready in: 4 h 30 m

Ingredients
- 4 cloves garlic, chopped
- 3 (29 ounce) cans tomato sauce
- 4 (6 ounce) cans tomato paste
- 1 tablespoon chopped fresh parsley
- 1 tablespoon chopped fresh basil
- 2 pounds ground beef
- 1 pound ground pork
- 1 cup dry bread crumbs
- 1 cup grated Parmesan cheese
- 1 teaspoon garlic powder
- 1 tablespoon chopped fresh parsley

Direction
- In a large pot mix together garlic, tomato sauce, tomato paste, parsley and basil. Bring sauce to a boil and then turn down the heat and simmer.
- In a large bowl mix together the ground beef, ground pork, bread crumbs, parmesan cheese, garlic powder and parsley. Shape into balls the size of a child's fist. In a skillet, fry meatballs in hot olive oil

until brown. Add to sauce mixture. Simmer over low heat for four hours.

Nutrition Information
- Calories: 233 calories
- Total Fat: 11.3 g
- Cholesterol: 46 mg
- Sodium: 1044 mg
- Total Carbohydrate: 17.4 g
- Protein: 17.3 g

Oxtail Ragu

"Richly browned oxtail sections are simmered low and slow in a rich tomato sauce until the meat comes off the bones-- this oxtail ragu is almost foolproof. The only way to screw up this incredibly succulent cut of beef is to not cook it long enough."

Serving: 4 | Prep: 15 m | Cook: 4 h 45 m | Ready in: 5 h

Ingredients
- 3 1/2 pounds beef oxtail, cut into 2-inch sections
- 1 tablespoon olive oil
- Salt and freshly ground black pepper
- 1 large yellow onion, diced
- 6 cloves garlic, roughly chopped
- 1/4 cup sherry vinegar
- 4 cups tomato sauce or puree, or more if desired
- 2 cups chicken broth, or enough to cover the oxtails
- 1 sprig fresh rosemary
- 2 sprigs fresh thyme
- 2 sprigs fresh oregano
- 1 teaspoon kosher salt, plus more to taste
- 1/4 teaspoon red chili flakes

Direction
- Preheat oven to 425 degrees F (220 degrees C). Lightly oil a baking pan large enough to hold the oxtails in a single layer.
- Place chopped onions and garlic in prepared pan. Rub oxtail sections with olive oil; season with salt

and freshly ground black pepper. Arrange on top of onions. Roast in preheated oven for 25 minutes. Turn oxtails and continue roasting until well browned, another 20 to 35 minutes. Remove pan from oven.
- Pour in wine vinegar, tomato sauce, chicken stock or water, rosemary, thyme, oregano, salt, and red chili flakes to the baking pan; stir. Pour the entire mixture into a large pot. Place over medium-high heat until sauce begins to simmer. Cover; reduce heat, and simmer over low heat until meat easily separates from the bone and is very tender, about 4 to 5 hours. Skim off fat before serving.

Nutrition Information
- Calories: 607 calories
- Total Fat: 30.8 g
- Cholesterol: 221 mg
- Sodium: 3307 mg
- Total Carbohydrate: 19.2 g
- Protein: 65.1 g

Papas Tomato Sauce

"My father's recipe for tomato sauce that the entire extended family loved."

Serving: 8 | Prep: 20 m | Cook: 4 h 42 m | Ready in: 5 h 2 m

Ingredients
- 1/4 cup olive oil

- 1 cup chopped red onion
- 1/2 cup chopped fresh parsley
- 1 1/2 tablespoons dried basil
- 2 cloves garlic, chopped
- 1/2 pound pork neck bones
- 1/2 pound beef neck bones
- 2 (28 ounce) cans crushed tomatoes
- 1 3/4 tablespoons salt
- 1 tablespoon dried oregano
- 2 bay leaves
- 1 (6 ounce) can tomato paste

Direction

- Heat olive oil in a large pot over medium heat. Add onion, parsley, basil, and garlic; cook and stir until onions are soft, about 5 minutes. Add pork and beef neck bones; cook and stir until browned, 7 to 10 minutes.
- Stir crushed tomatoes slowly into the onion mixture; mix in salt, oregano, and bay leaves. Cook, covered, until flavors combine, about 2 1/2 hours. Stir in tomato paste; simmer uncovered until sauce thickens, about 2 hours.

Nutrition Information

- Calories: 239 calories
- Total Fat: 15.5 g
- Cholesterol: 17 mg
- Sodium: 1966 mg
- Total Carbohydrate: 21.4 g
- Protein: 7.9 g

Pasta Sauce a la Pauly

"Enjoy this meaty pasta sauce over your favorite noodles."

Serving: 6 | Prep: 15 m | Cook: 3 h 10 m | Ready in: 3 h 25 m

Ingredients
- 1 cup butter
- 1 tablespoon extra-virgin olive oil
- 1/4 pound ground veal
- 1/4 pound ground beef
- 1/4 pound ground pork
- 2 (19 ounce) cans stewed tomatoes
- 1 1/2 (6 ounce) cans tomato paste
- 1 onion, chopped
- 1/2 pound sliced fresh mushrooms
- 1/2 cup red wine
- 1/2 green bell pepper, chopped
- 4 cloves garlic, minced
- 1 1/2 teaspoons white sugar
- 1/2 teaspoon Worcestershire sauce
- 1/2 teaspoon bitters (such as Angostura®)
- 1 pinch cayenne pepper

Direction
- Melt butter with the olive oil in a pot over medium heat. Cook and stir veal, beef, and pork in the butter

mixture until completely browned, about 10 minutes.
- Stir stewed tomatoes, tomato paste, onion, mushrooms, red wine, bell pepper, garlic, sugar, Worcestershire sauce, bitters, and cayenne pepper into the meat mixture; bring to a simmer, reduce heat to medium-low, and cook at a simmer until the tomatoes break down into a sauce, at least 3 hours.

Nutrition Information
- Calories: 568 calories
- Total Fat: 44 g
- Cholesterol: 127 mg
- Sodium: 999 mg
- Total Carbohydrate: 28.3 g
- Protein: 15.6 g

Pasta Sauce with Italian Sausage

"A flavorful homemade recipe for those who are tired of sweet pasta sauces. Serve over your favorite pasta with a tossed green salad and crusty garlic bread."

Serving: 6 | Prep: 30 m | Cook: 1 h | Ready in: 1 h 30 m

Ingredients
- 1 pound Italian sausage links
- 1/2 pound lean ground beef
- 1 tablespoon olive oil
- 1 onion, chopped

- 1 clove garlic, chopped
- 1 (16 ounce) can canned tomatoes
- 1 (15 ounce) can canned tomato sauce
- 1 teaspoon salt
- 1/4 teaspoon ground black pepper
- 1 teaspoon dried basil
- 1 teaspoon dried oregano
- 1 bay leaf

Direction

- Removed casing from sausage links and cut into 1/2 inch slices. In a large skillet, brown sausage over medium heat for about 10 minutes; remove and set aside.
- In a large skillet, heat ground beef, olive oil, garlic and onion over medium heat until meat is nicely browned; drain.
- Pour in tomatoes and tomato sauce; mix in salt, ground black pepper, basil, oregano, bay leaf and cooked sausage. Simmer uncovered for 1 hour, stirring occasionally.
- Bring a large pot of lightly salted water to a boil. Add pasta and cook for 8 to 10 minutes or until al dente; drain.
- Mix cooked sauce with hot pasta and remove bay leaf from sauce before serving.

Nutrition Information

- Calories: 339 calories
- Total Fat: 24.6 g
- Cholesterol: 58 mg
- Sodium: 1518 mg

- Total Carbohydrate: 11.4 g
- Protein: 18.5 g

Pork and Shiitake Mushroom Ragu

"Italian, paleo, omg, ragù! This was simply amazing. We are at our lake house for the summer and our friends came over. I had a super busy day and while at the butcher deciding what to make, the pork butt looked amazing.

I did serve this dish with a creamy polenta. I am Italian! What can I say... if you want to keep it paleo, then serve with sauteed vegetables or sauteed garlic spinach (I do that a lot).
 This freezes well and taste even better the next day! You can also prepare this meal in your slow cooker."

Serving: 8 | Prep: 20 m | Cook: 3 h 40 m | Ready in: 4 h

Ingredients
- 3 pounds boneless pork shoulder (Boston Butt) roast, cut into chunks
- kosher salt and freshly ground pepper to taste
- 2 tablespoons olive oil
- 1 cup low-sodium chicken broth
- 4 cloves garlic, minced, or more to taste
- 1 tablespoon Italian seasoning
- 2 bay leaves

- 1 (28 ounce) can petite diced tomatoes
- 1 (6 ounce) can tomato paste, or more to taste
- 8 ounces shiitake mushrooms, sliced

Direction

- Season pork with kosher salt and pepper.
- Heat a large Dutch oven over medium-high heat; add oil. Stir pork into the hot oil and cooking, turning often with tongs, until pork is evenly browned, 10 to 12 minutes. Pour chicken broth over the pork and scrape any brown bits of food off the bottom of the Dutch oven using a wooden spoon; stir in garlic, Italian seasoning, and bay leaves.
- Mix tomatoes and tomato paste into pork mixture, stirring and pressing paste along the side of the Dutch oven to help dissolve it. Reduce heat to medium-low. Stir, cover, and cook for 2 1/2 hours.
- Remove Dutch oven from heat and shred pork into the tomato sauce using 2 forks. Add mushrooms; cover and simmer for 1 hour more. Remove bay leaves.

Nutrition Information

- Calories: 299 calories
- Total Fat: 19.6 g
- Cholesterol: 67 mg
- Sodium: 429 mg
- Total Carbohydrate: 10.5 g
- Protein: 20.2 g

ProscuittoShallot Vodka Sauce

"This vodka sauce was developed in a attempt to make a different Sunday dinner. It soon became the most requested dish I make."

Serving: 8 | Prep: 15 m | Cook: 15 m | Ready in: 30 m

Ingredients
- 1 tablespoon olive oil
- 1 (14.5 ounce) can whole tomatoes, chopped
- 1/2 pound prosciutto, chopped
- 1/2 cup diced shallots
- 1 pint heavy whipping cream
- 1/2 cup vodka
- salt and ground black pepper to taste

Direction
- Heat olive oil in a skillet over medium heat; cook and stir tomatoes, prosciutto, and shallots in hot oil until liquid cooks off, about 5 minutes. Add cream to shallot mixture; bring to a boil.
- Stir vodka into cream mixture, return to a boil while stirring constantly, reduce heat to low, and season with salt and pepper. Cover the skillet with a lid and cook until flavors blend, about 3 minutes. Remove from heat and let stand until sauce thickens slightly, about 3 minutes more.

Nutrition Information
- Calories: 375 calories
- Total Fat: 32.8 g
- Cholesterol: 106 mg

- Sodium: 665 mg
- Total Carbohydrate: 5.4 g
- Protein: 7.4 g

Ragu Bologna Pasta Sauce

"The word 'ragu' means to stimulate the appetite. This sauce certainly fits the bill and hails from Northern Italy. It does not use garlic, has just a touch of tomato paste and a sprinkling of grated nutmeg, too. The sauce may be used on ravioli, gnocchi, spaetzle or any other type of hot, cooked pasta."

Serving: 5

Ingredients
- 3/4 pound cubed flank steak
- 4 ounces ground pork
- 1/4 pound veal, trimmed and cubed
- 1/4 pound finely ground salt pork
- 1 onion, thinly sliced
- 1 carrot, sliced
- 1 stalk celery, chopped
- 1 1/4 cups chicken stock
- 1 teaspoon tomato paste
- 1/4 teaspoon salt
- 1/8 teaspoon ground black pepper
- 1/4 pound mushrooms, chopped
- 2 cooked chicken liver, diced
- 1/2 cup heavy whipping cream

- 1 small truffle, thinly sliced
- 1 pinch ground nutmeg

Direction

- In a large saucepan, combine beef, chopped pork, veal, salt pork, onion, carrot and celery to brown thoroughly over medium low heat. Add stock or water and continue to cook until it evaporates.
- Add tomato paste, salt, pepper and enough water to cover meat. Cover pan and cook slowly for 1 hour. Add mushrooms and livers and cook for 15 minutes longer. Just before serving add cream, truffle and nutmeg. Mix well and serve.

Nutrition Information

- Calories: 491 calories
- Total Fat: 39.6 g
- Cholesterol: 161 mg
- Sodium: 555 mg
- Total Carbohydrate: 5.3 g
- Protein: 27.7 g

Restaurant Style Spaghetti Sauce

"A delicious spaghetti sauce with red wine, Italian sausage, garlic and onions. The best I have ever had -- easy and delicious! Use a large, flat-bottomed saucepan so that the flavors can mingle."

Serving: 6 | Prep: 15 m | Cook: 45 m | Ready in: 1 h

Ingredients

- 1 tablespoon olive oil
- 1 onion, chopped
- 3 cloves garlic, minced
- 1 (28 ounce) can roma tomatoes (crushed)
- 1 (6 ounce) can tomato paste
- 1 cup Merlot wine
- 1 pound Italian sausage, sliced

Direction

- Heat olive oil in a large saucepan over medium heat. Sauté onion and garlic until tender and fragrant. Stir in crushed tomatoes, tomato paste and wine. Bring to a boil over medium-high heat.
- Reduce heat to low, stir in sausage and simmer until sausage is thoroughly cooked.

Nutrition Information

- Calories: 287 calories
- Total Fat: 16.8 g
- Cholesterol: 30 mg
- Sodium: 1043 mg
- Total Carbohydrate: 15.9 g
- Protein: 12.6 g

Ricks Tomato Gravy

"Easy preparation for a main course breakfast. Serve this sauce over hot halved biscuits."

Serving: 6 | Prep: 10 m | Cook: 25 m | Ready in: 35 m
Ingredients

- 4 slices bacon
- 3 tablespoons self-rising flour
- 2 cups water
- 1/4 teaspoon salt, or to taste
- 1 teaspoon ground black pepper, or to taste
- 1 (15 ounce) can diced tomatoes

Direction

- Place bacon in a large skillet and cook over medium-high heat, turning occasionally, until evenly browned, about 10 minutes. Remove bacon from pan, keeping the drippings in the skillet. Allow bacon to cool; crumble and return to bacon drippings.
- Stir flour into bacon and drippings over medium-high heat; cook and stir until flour is blended and lightly browned, 3 to 5 minutes. Slowly whisk water into flour mixture until thickened, about 5 minutes; season with salt and black pepper. Stir in tomatoes and simmer until gravy is cooked through, about 5 minutes. Serve over warmed biscuits.

Nutrition Information

- Calories: 112 calories
- Total Fat: 8.5 g
- Cholesterol: 13 mg
- Sodium: 405 mg
- Total Carbohydrate: 6.1 g
- Protein: 3.1 g

Sams Original Sauce

"An old recipe for sauce that was made by my grandfather's mother. Optional ingredients include pork chops, sausage, or ground pork."

Serving: 6 | Prep: 30 m | Cook: 6 h 20 m | Ready in: 6 h 50 m

Ingredients
- 1 yellow onion, chopped
- 1 tablespoon olive oil
- 4 cloves garlic, minced
- 1/2 pound cubed beef stew meat
- 4 tablespoons tomato paste
- 1 (28 ounce) can crushed tomatoes
- 1 pinch dried parsley
- 1 pinch dried basil
- 1 pinch fennel seed
- salt and pepper to taste

Direction
- Heat the oil in a large skillet over medium heat. Stir in the onion; cook and stir until the onion has softened and turned translucent, about 5 minutes. Reduce heat to medium-low, and continue cooking and stirring until the onion is very tender and dark brown, 15 to 20 minutes more. Add the garlic during the last 3 minutes of cooking.
- Transfer the onions and garlic to a bowl and set aside. Turn the heat up to medium high and add the beef cubes. Cook, stirring occasionally, until

browned on all sides, about 5 minutes. Drop in the tomato paste and reduce the heat to medium; allow the tomato paste to cook about 2 minutes, or until it begins to brown, before stirring.
- Pour in the crushed tomatoes and return the onions and garlic to the pan. Mix in the parsley, basil, fennel, and salt and pepper. Reduce the heat to low and simmer, stirring occasionally, until the sauce is thick and the meat is tender, 6 to 7 hours.

Nutrition Information
- Calories: 190 calories
- Total Fat: 9.7 g
- Cholesterol: 33 mg
- Sodium: 283 mg
- Total Carbohydrate: 14.3 g
- Protein: 13.3 g

Savory Italian Sausage Sauce

"This is a great homemade sauce. It's savory and spicy, as well as thick and chunky. The secret is the combination of Italian sausage, green onions, red wine and red pepper flakes. Easily double or triple amount and top on anything! Even better the next day. Enjoy."

Serving: 4 | Prep: 20 m | Cook: 1 h | Ready in: 1 h 20 m

Ingredients
- 2 tablespoons olive oil

- 4 cloves garlic, minced
- 1 pound Italian sausage
- 4 green onions, chopped
- 1 (8 ounce) package fresh mushrooms, sliced
- 1 tablespoon dried basil
- 1 tablespoon dried oregano
- 1 (15 ounce) can tomato sauce
- 1 (14.5 ounce) can stewed tomatoes
- 1 (6 ounce) can tomato paste
- 1/2 cup water
- 1/2 cup red wine
- 1 teaspoon red pepper flakes
- 2 tablespoons white sugar
- salt and pepper to taste

Direction

- Heat olive oil in a large skillet over medium-high heat. Sauté garlic until it browns. Place sausage in skillet with garlic. Cook until evenly brown, crumbling it as it cooks.
- Stir in mushrooms, basil and oregano; cook 5 minutes. Stir in tomato sauce, stewed tomatoes and tomato paste. Then add water, red wine, red pepper flakes and sugar. Season with salt and pepper to taste. Reduce heat to low and simmer for at least 1 hour.

Nutrition Information

- Calories: 495 calories
- Total Fat: 29.2 g
- Cholesterol: 45 mg

- Sodium: 2063 mg
- Total Carbohydrate: 36.3 g
- Protein: 21.1 g

Sicilian Ragu

"A great way to use your aging veggies! Freeze any unused sauce for later use. Can be served as a side dish with a green salad and meat, or by itself as a main dish. Serve with your favorite large pasta noodle. Penne works well!"

Serving: 8

Ingredients
- 1 pound lean ground beef
- 1 pound ground pork
- 1 onion, chopped
- 2 (14.5 ounce) cans diced tomatoes
- 4 cloves garlic, minced
- 2 carrots, diced
- 1 (15 ounce) can baby peas
- 1 cup water
- 1 bay leaf
- 1 tablespoon olive oil
- salt to taste

Direction
- In a large skillet cook ground beef, ground pork, and onion until brown.
- In a large saucepan mix together the tomatoes, garlic, carrots, peas, water, bay leaves, olive oil, and salt. Add meat mixture. Bring to a boil. Cover partially, and reduce to a simmer. Cook for one hour, stirring occasionally.

Nutrition Information
- Calories: 375 calories
- Total Fat: 25.6 g
- Cholesterol: 83 mg
- Sodium: 410 mg
- Total Carbohydrate: 11.3 g
- Protein: 22.5 g

Slow Cooker Bolognese

"A very thick and hearty meat sauce simmered in the slow cooker."

Serving: 8 | Prep: 20 m | Cook: 4 h 30 m | Ready in: 4 h 50 m

Ingredients
- 2 tablespoons olive oil
- 1 cup finely chopped baby carrots
- 1 onion, finely chopped
- 2 cloves garlic, minced
- 1 pound lean ground beef
- 1 cup whole milk
- 1 (28 ounce) can crushed tomatoes
- 1 (6 ounce) can tomato paste
- 1/2 teaspoon salt
- 1/2 teaspoon ground black pepper
- 1 teaspoon dried basil
- 1 teaspoon dried oregano
- 1/4 teaspoon crushed red pepper flakes

- 1/2 cup whole milk
- 1/4 cup grated Parmesan cheese

Direction

- Heat the olive oil in a large skillet over medium heat, and cook and stir the carrots, onion, and garlic until tender, about 10 minutes. Place the ground beef into the skillet and cook and stir, breaking up the meat as it cooks, until browned. Drain off excess fat from the skillet, and pour in 1 cup milk. Bring to a simmer, reduce heat to medium-low, and simmer until the milk is absorbed, about 15 minutes.
- Place the beef mixture into a slow cooker, and set the cooker to High. Stir in crushed tomatoes, tomato paste, salt, pepper, basil, oregano, and red pepper flakes, and cook for 2 hours. Mix in 1/2 cup milk and Parmesan cheese, stir well, and cook for 2 more hours.

Nutrition Information

- Calories: 245 calories
- Total Fat: 13 g
- Cholesterol: 44 mg
- Sodium: 547 mg
- Total Carbohydrate: 17.9 g
- Protein: 16.3 g

www.ingramcontent.com/pod-product-compliance
Lightning Source LLC
Chambersburg PA
CBHW071437070526
44578CB00001B/123